The MDS Self-Audit

A Practical Guide to Ensuring Minimum Data Set Accuracy

SECOND EDITION

Rena R. Shephard, MHA, RN, FACDONA, RAC-C

The MDS Self-Audit: A Practical Guide to Ensuring Minimum Data Set Accuracy, Second Edition is published by HCPro, Inc.

 5 4 3 2 1

ISBN 1-57839-764-2

Rena R. Shephard, MHA, RN, FACDONA, RAC-C, Author
Noelle Shough, Executive Editor
Paul Amos, Group Publisher
Julia Hopp, MS, RN, CNAA, BC, Reviewer
Jean St. Pierre, Director of Operations
Mike Michaud, Bookbuilder
Crystal Beland, Layout Artist
Laura Godinho, Cover Designer

Arrangements can be made for quantity discounts. For more information, contact

HCPro, Inc.
P.O. Box 1168
Marblehead, MA 01945
Telephone: 800/650-6787 or 781/639-1872
Fax: 781/639-2982
E-mail: *customerservice@hcpro.com*

Visit HCPro at its World Wide Web sites:
www.hcpro.com **and** ***www.hcmarketplace.com***

03/2006
20771

Contents

ACKNOWLEDGEMENTS

With the MDS now at the center of nursing home operations, it was important to me to produce this book to help providers to continuously improve care and documentation, as well as to receive the reimbursement they earn. Because of the many changes and updates to the regulations since the original publication of *The MDS Self- Audit: A Practical Guide to Ensuring Minimum Data Set Accuracy*, this second edition contains additional information, tools, and forms to assist with these critical auditing tasks.

For helping me to reach the point of being able to develop the expertise required to write this book, I would like to acknowledge my mentor from long ago, Louise Oberender, now with the Masonic Homes of California, who provided my first crash course in Medicare Part A and started me on this path.

My thanks also go to Sheila Banducci of Savvy Solutions for Senior Care in Walnut Creek, CA; Becky Carroll of HFS Consultants in Oakland, CA; Pam Manion and the MU MDS Quality and Research Team at the University of Missouri; Darla K. Watson, RN, president of Starpointe Healthcare Consulting in Springdale, AR; and Delores L. Galias, RN, RHIT, of Galias Consulting in Glendale, CA, for contributing auditing tools to this book.

To Diane Carter, president and chief executive officer of the American Association of Nurse Assessment Coordinators (AANAC), thank you for your support, your inspiration, and your friendship. And to my husband, Philip Fisch, and my daughter, April Medlin—none of this would happen without the support you give me every day.

Acknowledgement also must go to the members of the AANAC, who continue to educate me daily about what affects them and what matters to them out there in the field. They constantly inspire me to learn, to improve, and to find new ways to help them get their jobs done. Their dedication to their residents and to their job responsibilities never fails to amaze and delight me.

Introduction—Assessing the Quality of Care

The Resident Assessment Instrument and Minimum Data Set

Over the past 15 years, the Minimum Data Set (MDS) has become the center of life for nursing home providers. This federally mandated assessment tool, which started as one component in improving the quality of care by facilitating appropriate care planning, has taken center stage in reimbursement, survey and certification activities, and quality care monitoring.

The sweeping nursing home reform legislation that gave birth to the MDS was the Omnibus Budget Reconciliation Act of 1987 (OBRA '87). This act came in response to a call for reform following studies by the federal government that identified abuse, neglect, and inadequate care in nursing homes. It created minimum standards of care and established guaranteed rights for nursing home residents. Still in effect today, the OBRA '87 mandate to every nursing home was that "each resident must receive and the facility must provide the necessary care and services to attain or maintain the highest practicable physical, mental, and psychosocial well-being . . ." (42 CFR 483.25, F309).

To achieve this goal, as required by OBRA '87, nursing homes must conduct regular assessments to identify each resident's functional capacity and health status. The law specifies that these assessments must be comprehensive, accurate, standardized, and reproducible and that they must be completed initially and periodically thereafter according to a prescribed schedule. The tool for conducting these assessments, the Resident Assessment Instrument (RAI), is mandated by law and is required for all Medicare- and Medicaid-certified nursing homes.

The components of the RAI are as follows:

1. **The MDS:** The MDS is a screening tool that helps the assessor identify areas of functional and clinical status that might be problems, needs, or

strengths for a resident. Its core set of questions mandated by OBRA '87 focuses on a resident's functional status. Using a section of the MDS set aside for this purpose, individual states can add items as approved by the federal government. Go to *www.hcpro.com/content/43815.cfm* to download a blank copy of the MDS.

2. **Triggers:** Certain MDS items serve as red flags indicating possible problems or strengths, depending on the response to the item. These responses are referred to as "triggers." For example, if an item in item B5 (indicators of delirium—periodic disordered thinking/awareness) is coded as a "2" to indicate new onset or worsening, then delirium is triggered as a possible problem for this resident. However, if the items are coded as a "1" to indicate the behavior is present but not of recent onset, the item does not trigger.

3. **Resident Assessment Protocols (RAP):** When an MDS item triggers, it indicates the need for further, in-depth assessment of the triggered issue to determine whether it is a problem, need, or strength for the resident. The RAPs, which address 18 areas of functional status that represent some of the most common problems found on the care plans of nursing home residents, provide a framework for exploring the triggered issues by asking for additional data.

   This expanded assessment includes additional MDS item responses that may affect the problem, need, or strength, as well as information not collected on the MDS. Based on the results of the RAP analysis, a decision is made regarding whether the issue should be included in the care plan.

4. **RAP Summary:** Also known as Section V of the MDS, the RAP summary summarizes information about which RAPs are triggered and which RAPs are care planned. In addition, Section V must include documentation that points to the location and date of health record documentation that supports the decision to care plan or not to care plan each triggered item.

5. **Utilization Guidelines:** The guidelines provide detailed instructions on how to complete the RAI process, including the required schedule of assessments.

They are found in the current version of the MDS Version 2.0 *Long Term Care Facility Resident Assessment Instrument User's Manual.*

The MDS as a multifunctional tool

The RAI process was designed to help providers improve care in nursing homes through better assessment and care planning. Over the years, however, this assessment process has taken on many additional duties.

Quality indicators/quality measures and the survey process

Because the MDS is standardized, reproducible, and routinely transmitted to each state's database, it lends itself well to a national analytic reporting system that provides information about the outcomes of care in nursing homes. This system uses quality indicators/quality measures (QI/QM), which are indicators of outcome for 34 areas of care in nursing homes, to produce reports that describe and compare nursing homes on a national level and provide state- and facility-specific data. With the development of the current QI/QMs for this purpose, the MDS quickly became the focal point for licensing and certification surveys for long-term care facilities.

Each QI/QM is calculated based on responses to specific MDS items. If the response to an item indicates that the QI/QM is an issue for the resident, that resident's data will increase the facility's score for that QI/QM. For example, a resident will contribute to the QI/QM (prevalence of bladder or bowel incontinence) if the frequency of his or her incontinence is identified on the MDS as "3" (frequently incontinent) or "4" (incontinent) and if the resident does not have any of three conditions that would exclude him or her from the QI/QM. Residents with continence scored as "0" (continent), "1" (usually continent), or "2" (occasionally incontinent) will not contribute to the QI/QM score.

The national analytic reporting system provides summary reports for each facility, flagging any QI/QMs that fall above acceptable, preset thresholds and ranking facilities in comparison to state and national data. The system also provides detailed reports organized by resident, indicating which resident contributed to which QI/QMs.

Another report that is very helpful with a facility's quality improvement activities displays the trend for each QI/QM over time. Providers can access the reports through the

CASPER reporting system via their MDS transmission sites. Details regarding all 34 QI/QMs and the available reports can be found in the *Revised Facility Guide for the MDS QI/QM Reports* at *www.qtso.com/mdsdownload.html.*

As part of off-site, pre-survey activities they perform to prepare for licensing and certification surveys, surveyors access the QI/QM reports to identify issues of possible concern for use in the survey and to identify residents for possible focused review once the survey starts. However, the QI/QMs are not considered to be direct, accurate indicators of problems, and surveyors are instructed to verify QI/QM findings through record review, interviews, and direct observation once the survey begins.

The QI/QMs also should be an integral part of a facility's quality assessment and assurance committee activities to continuously improve the quality of care.

The revised survey process: The new Quality Indicator Survey

In 2005, CMS started a demonstration project in five states testing a revised survey process that has heavy emphasis on on-site automation, using data from several sources, including enhanced use of MDS data. Known as the Quality indicator Survey (QIS), the process employs 160 Quality Care Indicators (QCI), including 44 that are derived from the MDS. The 24 Quality Indicators originally used in the current survey process are included in the 44 MDS QCIs.

Here are some pertinent facts about the QIS, according to an October 2005 Survey & Certification Letter to surveyors from CMS:

- The QIS was designed as a staged process for use by surveyors to systematically and objectively review all regulatory areas and subsequently focus on selected areas for further review.

- The QIS provides a structure for an initial review of larger samples of residents based on the MDS, observations, interviews, and medical record reviews. Using on-site automation, survey findings from the first stage are combined to provide rates on a comprehensive set of QCIs covering all resident- and facility-level federal regulations for nursing homes. The second stage then provides surveyors the opportunity to focus survey resources on further investigation of care areas where concerns exist. Although the survey process has been revised under the QIS, the federal regulations and interpretive guidance remain unchanged (S&C-06-02).

- According to training materials for the survey's demonstration project, survey data will be derived from three sources:

    - **An MDS sample,** which includes all residents with an MDS assessment within the past six months of the survey
    - **A census sample,** which reflects a random sample of current residents (n=40)
    - **An admission sample,** which contains a random sample of new admissions (n=30)

  Surveyors also may initiate a sample at their discretion.

Additional information on the QIS can be found at *www.uchsc.edu/hcpr/slides/slideIndex.html*. The QIS training manual can be found at *www.aging.state.ks.us/Manuals/QISManual.htm*.

Quality measures and consumer interest

With implementation of the Nursing Home Quality Initiative and the publicly reported quality measures (QM) in 2002, the MDS became the link between resident care outcomes and consumers. Like the QI/QMs, the QMs are derived from MDS data depending on the responses to designated MDS items. Over time, these outcome measures have been incorporated into the QI/QMs used in the survey process.

Facility-specific scores for the QMs are posted on the Internet at *www.medicare.gov*, along with state and national comparison information. The Web site offers residents, family members, and other potential consumers the ability to sort the information by facility name, ZIP code, and other geographic parameters. As a result, the QMs provide a market-driven incentive for providers to improve nursing home care. Details about the QMs can be found at *www.cms.hhs.gov/NursingHomeQualityInits/*.

Like the QI/QMs, the QMs should be an integral part of the facility's continuous quality improvement activities.

Resource Utilization Groups and Medicare reimbursement

The MDS determines Medicare Part A reimbursement under the extended care benefit for skilled nursing facilities (SNF). Since the advent of the SNF Prospective Payment System (PPS) in 1998, resident-specific MDS responses have been used to predict resident needs and resource utilization in dollar amounts. This information is used to classify residents into Resource Utilization Groups (RUG), each of which defines the level of care residents require. Medicare then reimburses for each resident based on that defined level of care.

This connection with reimbursement is possible because the MDS contains items that reflect the acuity level of the resident, including diagnoses, treatments, and evaluations of the resident's functional status. Although the MDS is the foundation for this payment system, it is not only the MDS data that determines reimbursement. Each resident's health record must provide documentation to support the MDS responses and reflect that a medically necessary daily skilled service was provided.

Many states have opted to use a similar case-mix reimbursement system for Medicaid. Regardless of the purpose of the MDS assessment, however, if it is to be transmitted to the state database, the assessment must comply with federal regulations, including the federal MDS coding rules.

The need for MDS accuracy

Although the key to achieving favorable survey results, good QI/QM scores, and good QM scores lies in using resident care systems that produce positive resident outcomes, even the best resident care will not result in favorable scores if the assessments that underlie the MDS data are not accurate. Similarly, if RUGs are based on inaccurate MDS data, they likely will not reflect the true intensity of care provided. Thus, nursing homes have a considerable stake in ensuring the accuracy of their MDS data.

State and federal governments have stakes in MDS accuracy, too. The federal government needs accurate MDS data because it is responsible for the SNF PPS payment system and for the quality of care delivered in certified facilities. Without good data, it can't fulfill its responsibilities. In states where Medicaid payment is based on MDS data, states have a direct interest in correct assessments as well. Consequently, several state and federal agencies monitor MDS accuracy.

MDS accuracy is also monitored by surveyors as a part of the survey process. Additionally, the federal Office of Inspector General, the policing arm of Medicare, has published several reports identifying problems with MDS accuracy, as has the Government Accountability Office.

DAVE reviews

In order to monitor MDS accuracy on a continuing basis, CMS began the Data Accuracy and Verification (DAVE) project in 2004. Focusing on MDS assessments and consequent claims, DAVE had several objectives: According to CMS, DAVE was meant to check the correctness of MDS assessment data, encourage facilities to initiate quality of care improvements, support CMS' efforts to pay facilities accurately for care provided, and help CMS further develop its payment policies.

The DAVE reviewers compiled information on data accuracy via on-site visits to a small number of SNFs as well as through off-site reviews of records requested from providers. Although this project ended after a year and a half, much significant information came out of the project and is summarized on p. xiv.

The government restarted the DAVE project in the spring of 2006, dubbing the revamped MDS auditing method "DAVE2." For DAVE2, CMS is using MDS-proficient nurses who are conducting onsite MDS accuracy probes at the rate of 30 facilities per quarter nationwide. The purposes of DAVE2 are threefold, according to a report from the Office of Inspector General:

1. To assess the accuracy and reliabilty of MDS coding answers

2. To develop methods of further MDS accuracy testing
3. To improve MDS accuracy through pertinent training for state RAI coordinators, MDS coordinators and other facility staff, state surveyors, and fiscal intermediaries

CMS has big plans for the data it will reap from DAVE2 reviewers. It plans to use the MDS data to form future assessment tools, refine and develop more quality measures, and of course, improve the quality of care given in nursing homes.

Important for nursing homes to know is that DAVE2 reviewers won't take the same focus on reimbursement items that they did in the past. The government says it wants to improve MDS coding rather than penalize facilities financially for inaccurate MDSs. However, it's likely that if a DAVE2 review uncovered a serious quality of care issue, the reviewer would have to report it to the state to initiate a complaint survey.

According to CMS, these are the top MDS discrepancy items it found during the DAVE beta test review:

Common discrepancies in off-site reviews:

1. P8—physician orders
2. O1—number of medications
3. P7—physician visits
4. P1bcB—physical therapy, total number of minutes
5. P1bbB—occupational therapy, total number of minutes
6. I1nn—allergies
7. O3—injections, number of days
8. P1bcA—physical therapy, number of days
9. P1bbA—occupational therapy, number of days
10. G1hA—eating, self-performance
11. O4e—diuretic
12. P5—hospital stays
13. O4c—antidepressants
14. I1h—hypertension

Common discrepancies in on-site reviews of Medicaid:

1. O1—number of medications
2. P8—physician orders
3. K2b—weight in pounds
4. B4—cognitive skills for daily decision-making
5. P7—physician visits
6. G1hA—eating, self-performance
7. G1bA—transfer, self-performance
8. G1iA—toilet use, self-performance
9. G1iB—toilet use, support provided
10. J2a—pain frequency
11. G1jA—personal hygiene, self-performance
12. G1fA—locomotion off unit, self-performance
13. G1hB—eating, support provided
14. G1aA—bed mobility, self-performance

Common discrepancies when DAVE reviewers completed an MDS assessment after a facility nurse completed an assessment on same Medicare resident:

1. O1—number of medications
2. P8—physician orders
3. J2a—pain frequency
4. A9f—patient responsible for self
5. K2b—weight in pounds
6. J5d—stability of conditions, none of the above
7. P2e—reorientation (i.e., cueing)
8. Q2—overall change in care needs
9. L1c—some/all natural teeth lost
10. J2b—pain intensity
11. P7—physician visits
12. I1nn—allergies

13. J1n—unsteady gait
14. P1ae—monitoring acute medical condition

Items in Sections P and O had the most discrepancies in all types of DAVE reviews, according to information from CMS. Review the coding tips in the next chapter to master coding these problematic items.

As a result of the evolution of the MDS and its multiple uses, as well as the increased scrutiny of MDS data by the government, the role of MDS auditing in SNFs should move to the top of the priority list for providers.

Chapter 1

THE CHALLENGES OF MDS CODING

The MDS coding rules guide assessors to collect specific information that the government uses for precise purposes. The item-by-item guide to the MDS in Chapter 3 of the *Long Term Care Facility Resident Assessment Instrument User's Manual* gives the authoritative instructions for completing each item on the form.

Because the MDS drives such disparate functions as care planning, QI/QMs, publicly reported QMs, RUGs, and the survey process, the coding rules are somewhat complex. Sometimes the goal of the coding is to identify the resident's functional status. For example, when coding MDS item G1bA, activities of daily living (ADL) self-performance for transfers, the instructions say to code the resident at the highest level of dependence that occurred three or more times in the observation period (read further in this chapter for important details about coding item G1). In this case, the coding decision is likely to represent the resident's functional status.

However, sometimes an item looks at functional status, but its goal is to provide information about resource utilization. In such a case, the coding rules might not be as clinically intuitive or representative of the resident's functional status. For example, in the case of G1b, transfer (as well as all items in G1A), if the transfer activity takes place fewer than three times, the item is coded "0," independent, regardless of the level of assistance required for the one or two transfers that did take place. Because G1b, transfer, is one of the four ADL activities used to calculate the RUG levels, that coding rule for this item focuses more on the payment perspective. In other words, if the resident's activity status does not reach a certain level (i.e., occurring three or more times), then fewer resources (i.e., staff time) are utilized and the coding rules prevent the payment level from increasing on the basis of that activity.

Because of such complexities, everyone with a role in coding the MDS must master the coding rules related to the items for which they are responsible. To assist with that mastery—and to avoid errors in the first place, which is the first line of defense in MDS accuracy—this section contains a review of the most common coding errors and the most common causes of those errors.

Section G—Physical functioning and structural problems

Item G1A, ADL self-performance, is significantly prone to error. It has direct implications for care planning, the QMs, the QI/QMs, and PPS reimbursement. Coding errors for this item occur for the following reasons:

Poor understanding of ADL activity definitions

Each of these items has a very specific definition, often including a list of subtasks to be considered when making the coding decision. Assessors must be careful to include in the assessment all listed subtasks—and not to include subtasks that are not listed.

For example, bed mobility, item G1a, includes how the resident moves to and from a lying position, turns side to side, and positions his or her own body while in bed, a recliner, or other type of furniture in which the resident sleeps. Coding errors often occur because assessors tend to think of bed mobility as the resident turning side to side and positioning his or her own body in bed, and they forget to take into consideration the resident's ability to move to and from a lying position.

Another common error involves the perceived overlap between the tasks involved in bed mobility and transfer, item G1b. A transfer from one surface to another begins after the resident is positioned and ready for transfer. Therefore, sitting up on the bed and moving the legs over the side of the bed do not count in coding transfers—they are included in bed mobility. The transfer itself is defined as how the resident moves between surfaces (i.e., to and from bed, chair, wheelchair, standing position.) Movements to and from bath or toilet are excluded from this item.

Some of these ADL items also specify the activity's location. For example, sometimes providers miscode item G1c, walk in room, by including walking that occurs in the physical therapy room or in the hall. On the other hand, information for G1b, transfers, would be collected from all sources because the item definition does not limit the activity's location. If the item definition does not specify location, then information should be collected about the resident's performance at all locations.

Lack of expertise in the complex ADL coding rules

The rules for coding ADLs require collecting information from all possible sources—certified nursing assistants (CNA) caring for the resident, rehabilitation therapists involved with the resident, family members, significant others, other staff, and volunteers, unless otherwise indicated in the *Long Term Care Facility Resident Assessment Instrument User's Manual* instructions. Often, providers go wrong when they depend on only a few sources of information, rather than all possible sources.

Once all of the relevant information is collected, coding decisions for each ADL in item G1 must be made to determine whether the resident's status is independent (code "0"), has supervision (code "1"), receives limited assistance (code "2"), receives extensive assistance (code "3"), has total dependence (code "4"), or the activity did not occur (code "8"). In general, the coding rules require that the resident is coded at the most dependent level of care that occurred three or more times in the observation period.

Coding errors often occur when assessors don't understand the difference between limited assistance and extensive assistance. See the tip box on p. 4 for more information.

To code an activity as *independent*, the resident must perform all aspects of the activity without assistance. Caregiver help or oversight may occur one or two times and the activity can still be counted as independent, but once caregiver assistance occurs a third time, the activity can no longer be coded as independent. A resident is also coded as independent in an activity if the activity itself occurred a total of only one or two times in the observation period, regardless of the level of assistance provided.

To code an activity as *supervision*, the resident would receive non-physical assistance (i.e., oversight, encouragement, or cueing) as the most dependent level of assistance that occurred three or more times in the observation period. Physical assistance could occur one or two times, and the activity would still be coded at the supervision level.

Limited assistance refers to physical assistance in guided maneuvering of limbs or other non weight-bearing assistance. If this is the most dependent level of assistance provided three or more times in the observation period, then the activity would be coded as limited assistance, even if a higher level of physical assistance (e.g., weight-bearing assistance) occurred one or two times.

Consistent with the previous coding instructions, *extensive assistance* is defined as weight-bearing support provided three or more times. This definition also includes full caregiver performance of an activity three or more times during part but not all of the observation period. An item also is coded at this level if the staff or other caregiver performed an entire subtask of the activity three or more times in the observation period.

The coding rules for *total dependence* vary somewhat from the rules described above. To code an activity as a "4," caregivers must have performed all aspects of the activity for the entire observation period, with complete nonparticipation by the resident.

Coding that does not reflect the resident's actual performance

The coding instructions require that the MDS data reflect what the resident actua does, as opposed to what caregivers believe the resident is capable of or aspires to. example, a resident's wife visits at mealtimes throughout the day and feeds the reside Staff believe that the resident is capable of some self-feeding activities, but their recommendations for a feeding retraining program have been declined by the resident and his wife. In coding G1h, eating, this resident would be coded as "4," total dependence.

Another example is the resident who is very slow in dressing herself, even with task segmentation, but who has demonstrated that she can dress herself with cueing. The CNA encourages her at the beginning of the activity but, due to time constraints, actually performs much of the activity for the resident. This resident would be coded at the extensive assistance level (code "3") despite her actual capabilities.

Inconsistency regarding the lookback period

One of the most common errors is inconsistency in the assessment reference date (ARD) among disciplines. The ARD represents the end of the observation period for all sections of a particular MDS assessment. As such, it defines the care and services that are captured on the MDS. Although different sections of the MDS may require looking back at different numbers of days, depending on the MDS section, all must end on the ARD. Therefore, when members of the interdisciplinary team use different ARDs in their assessments, significant inaccuracies occur.

Cutting the lookback period short

Even when all team members use the same ARD, errors occur when assessors fail to account for the entire observation period. For example, this can happen when a team member completes an item prior to the ARD. Because the ARD marks the end of the observation period, important information can be missed in the time period between completion of the item and the ARD. Similarly, if an item is completed on the ARD, important data may be missed after the item is completed and before the end of that particular day.

o fall short if information is not gathered from all shifts A common error is to use certified nursing assistant (CNA) of information in making coding decisions for Section G.

port or to facilitate coding

provide enough information to support the coding deci- ns. How the facility decides to document that information is up to . If the health record does not support the coding, it might be because infor- mation on ADL activities in the record is sparse and the assessor made the coding decision based on data that were not written in the record.

Another cause of coding errors is failure to account for all available information to make the coding decision. For example, if CNAs use flowsheets for ADL documentation, they represent only one source of information. Another potential source of information is documentation provided by nurses, rehabilitation therapists, physicians, and other interdisciplinary team members. Admission and quarterly skin, bowel and bladder, and fall assessments also contain details about ADL status. In addition, care plans may be a source of ADL data.

A common source of difficulty when it comes to coding this MDS item is translation of the documentation by rehabilitation therapists. Generally, rehabilitation therapists utilize functional independence measures (FIM) to rate a resident's functional abilities. The following chart, Figure 1.1, can assist with that translation.

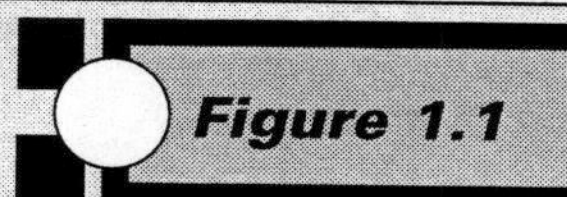

Figure 1.1

FIM to MDS ADL code conversion chart

FIM		MDS	
Complete independence Modified independence	7.0 6.0	Independent	0
Supervision/contact	5.0	Supervision	1
Minimal assistance	4.0	Limited assistance	2
Moderate assistance	3.0	Extensive assistance	3
Maximum assistance Complete dependence	2.0 1.0	Total dependence	4

Source: Chart use courtesy of Delores L. Galias, RN, RHIT of Galias Consulting in Glendale, CA. Reprinted with permission.

The coding instructions recognize that residents perform at varying levels of dependence depending on the time of day, their overall health status, which discipline is involved, and other variables. Consequently, it is not necessary that all sources of information in the health record be in agreement with regard to ADL performance. For example, residents generally do better with physical therapy in the daytime than they do with nursing staff in the middle of the night. This variability must be taken into consideration when making the MDS coding decision, and the seemingly contradictory chart documentation is appropriate.

Unresolved inconsistencies, however, are cause for concern. For example, if the CNAs document that the resident ambulates without assistance to the bathroom throughout each day and night, but physical therapy documents that the resident requires limited to extensive assistance for gait training during the entire observation period, that inconsistency should be explained in the chart.

Variability in coding among MDS coders within the facility

When it was developed, the MDS was required to be standardized and reproducible. That requirement implies that multiple assessors completing the same item should agree on the same coding decision. However, when all assessors in the facility do not have the same level of understanding of the process or the same expertise in coding, however, variability occurs between assessments.

For example, when one assessor completes a five-day MDS assessment and a second assessor with a different understanding of the ADL coding rules completes the 14-day assessment, the resulting RUG scores may differ even though the resident's status has not actually changed. This issue also has implications for care planning, QI/QMs, and QMs. Take the case of a resident whose ADL status is calculated for the quality measure Residents Whose Need for Help with Daily Activities has increased by comparing the current assessment to the most recent prior assessment. If the assessors who coded the two assessments do not have the same understanding of the coding rules, the resident's status might be reported as declining or improving when in fact it is unchanged.

Section E1—Indicators of depression, anxiety, sad mood

Depression is a condition that is under diagnosed and under treated in the elderly. A RAP as well as some QI/QMs and QMs focus on this problem because of its implications for the resident's functional status, overall health, and quality of life. In addition, the RUG reimbursement system recognizes when a resident meets a specified definition of depression and classifies the resident into a higher reimbursement level.

Coding errors in this section are attributable to several factors:

An indicator listed in E1a through E1p must be coded even if it occurred only once in the 30-day observation period

The coding rules are to code "0," indicator not exhibited in past 30 days, if the indicator did not occur at all. An indicator should be coded "1" if it occurred at least once during the 30-day observation period but less than on six days a week. If the indicator occurred on six or more days per week, it would be coded "2."

Interpretation of the coding rules

In the *Long Term Care Facility Resident Assessment Instrument User's Manual*, the intent of item E1 is "to record the frequency of indicators observed in the past 30 days, irrespective of the assumed cause of the indicator (behavior)." The coding section reiterates, "Remember, code regardless of what you believe the cause to be."

However, variations in coding these items continue to occur due to variations in the presumed cause. For example, item E1m is crying/tearfulness. Even if a resident cried because she was watching a sad movie, a strict interpretation of the coding rules would indicate that this episode of crying should be coded in E1m. But some assessors argue that the title of E1, indicators of depression, anxiety, sad mood, would exclude crying due to a sad movie.

Another example is the resident who requests PRN, or "as needed," medication several times per day. Should he be coded at E1h, repetitive health complaints? The examples provided in the manual for this item are "persistently seeks medical attention, obsessive concern with body functions."

The keys to overcoming these pitfalls lie in being familiar with all item definitions and adopting a strict interpretation of the instructions. When it comes to determining whether a resident meets the definition for repetitive health complaints, repetitive verbalizations, and other indicators that do not have clear black-and-white definitions, facilities should adopt practices that are justifiable and that ensure consistency among their own assessors.

Contradictory information between disciplines, the chart, and the MDS

One of the major pitfalls here is the failure of the assessor to account for information from all team members, family, volunteers, and others involved with the resident's care. For example, a social worker who was assigned to complete item E1 asserted that he would code based only on firsthand knowledge. Consequently, indicators that occurred on the night shift and weekends were not represented in the coding.

Generally, the rule of thumb is that a clinician should document only what he or she has witnessed firsthand. However, the *Long Term Care Facility Resident Assessment Instrument User's Manual* is clear in its instructions that the coding decision must be made based on input by all caregivers across all shifts for the entire observation period.

Care and documentation systems that fail to identify new symptoms

Unless the facility sets up clear lines of communication and documentation, symptoms that appear after the initial identification of a problem may evade the formal monitoring process and, as a result, not be represented on the MDS.

To avoid such a situation, assessors should not rely solely on behavior-monitoring flow sheets for their information. In preparation for making the coding decisions for item E1, as with other items, they should consult documentation by all shifts and disciplines and conduct interviews with interdisciplinary team members to ensure the accuracy of the data used for coding decisions.

Section I—Disease diagnoses

To code diseases in item I1 and infections in item I2, they must relate to the resident's current ADL, cognitive, mood, or behavior status; medical treatments; nursing monitoring; or risk of death. One of the most common errors for this section is including diseases and infections when they are not relevant to current functioning or to the current care plan.

For example, consider a resident with a history of hypertension who has never required medications to control blood pressure, and only routine monitoring of vital signs is indicated. Therefore, hypertension should not be checked at I1h. Similarly, for the resident with a history of a hip fracture that is well-healed and no longer presents a problem for the resident in any way, the hip fracture should not be coded at item I1m.

For item I2, infections, only the infection itself should be coded in relation to the resident's current status. The sequelae of infections (e.g., decreased endurance and functional decline) should not be included here. This item is often overcoded because of errors related to this issue.

Coding errors are also very common for item I2j, urinary tract infections (UTI), and result in inappropriate elevation of the UTI QI/QM and the corresponding quality measure. This problem is attributable to the precise definition for UTI, which some clinicians see as counterintuitive. For this item, acute and chronic UTIs must be coded, and all of the following criteria must be met during the 30-day observation period:

The resident must be symptomatic

Symptoms include the common manifestations of a UTI (e.g, burning during urination or urinary urgency or frequency). In cognitively impaired residents, it is often difficult to identify these symptoms. However, these residents often exhibit changes in behavior, increased agitation, or other symptoms that alert nursing staff to the possibility of an infection and should stimulate further investigation. Any such symptoms would meet the intent of this item.

To code this item, the symptoms must occur during at least part of the 30-day observation period. If no symptoms occurred during this lookback period, this item should not be coded, even if the resident is taking antibiotics for a UTI and some or all of the other criteria are met.

Significant laboratory findings must be in the health record

Significant laboratory findings include a urinalysis and a culture and sensitivity test. It is not required that such laboratory tests be completed during the observation period. Rather, this item can be checked if the laboratory tests were completed prior to the observation period but the resident was symptomatic during at least part of the observation period—and all of the other criteria are met.

This item also may be coded if the resident meets the other criteria and the physician gives a working diagnosis of UTI based on pending laboratory tests. However, if the laboratory test results later indicate that a UTI is not present, a correction should be processed to remove the UTI from the MDS.

A physician's diagnosis must appear in the chart

It is not necessary that the physician actually write the diagnosis during the observation period. As long as the other criteria are met for coding this item, if the infection was diagnosed prior to the observation period and documented in the record by the physician, the physician does not have to write the diagnosis again.

The record must reflect current supporting documentation of all of the above

Section J—Health conditions

In Section J1, Problem conditions, several MDS items are vulnerable to error. Item J1c, dehydrated: output exceeds intake, is among those items. To check J1c, two out of three indicators must be present. Therefore, this item is not based on a physician diagnosis—it must be coded based on the signs and symptoms listed in the instructions.

Item J1h, fever, should be coded when the resident's temperature is 2.4 degrees greater than baseline, according to the *Long Term Care Facility Resident Assessment Instrument User's Manual* coding instructions. Although a clinical practice standard for establishing the baseline temperature has not yet been set in the long-term care industry, each facility should develop its own procedure for establishing a baseline temperature for residents and follow that procedure consistently. The procedure should also include instructions to nursing staff on how to identify fever before the resident's baseline temperature has been established.

A word about pain

Item J2, pain symptoms, is frequently miscoded. Coding for this section should be based on physical assessment of the resident's pain, direct observation of the resident, and discussions with the resident about his or her pain status. Information should be collected across all disciplines and shifts for the entire seven-day observation period.

Assessors must avoid judging a resident's statements about his or her pain, adopting the principle that pain is what the resident says it is. However, assessors must also note the resident's nonverbal indicators of pain, such as grimacing, guarding a part of the body, and other such expressions and behaviors, especially because some residents cannot express themselves or are stoic and do not want to complain or "bother" the staff.

Based on the information collected, the first question is whether the resident had pain during the observation period, regardless of the cause and regardless of pain management efforts. If the answer is yes, item J5a should be coded according to the frequency of the pain: For pain less than daily, code "1," and for pain daily, code "2" (the code "0" indicates no pain).

The next question is, of all of the pain experienced by the resident during the observation period, what is the highest level of intensity that occurred, even if it happened only once? Item J2b, intensity of pain, should be coded as mild, moderate, or horrible or excruciating based on that answer. For facilities that use a pain intensity scale of 0–10, with "0" indicating no pain and "10" indicating the highest intensity of pain that the resident can imagine, a recommended crosswalk to the MDS pain scale would be as follows:

- Pain levels 1, 2, and 3 are coded as mild pain
- Pain levels 4, 5, and 6 are coded as moderate pain
- Pain levels 7, 8, 9, and 10 are coded as horrible or excruciating pain

This method is based on the University of Iowa Gerontological Nursing Interventions Research Dissemination Core's evidence-based protocol, "Acute Pain Management in the Elderly." Go to *www.nursing.uiowa.edu/centers/gnirc/protocols.htm* to order a copy of the protocol. Also see the algorithms on the Medicare Quality Improvement Web site by going to *www.medqic.org* and typing "pain algorithms" in the search box.

Studies indicate that the responses for item J3, pain site, are often not well-supported by health record documentation. Thorough and accurate pain assessments can help to reduce the occurrence of this error. In addition, the nurse administering pain medication should clearly identify the location of the pain and avoid making assumptions about it based on previous assessments.

A word about falls

Regarding item J4, accidents, the debate about the definition of a fall has been persistent and at times heated. Some providers may try to parse the definition to avoid capturing falls that should be coded in item J4a, fell in past 30 days, but splitting hairs with the definitions can cause lapses in the care plan.

A fall can generally be defined as an unexpected or unintended movement from a surface to a lower surface. The *Long Term Care Facility Resident Assessment Instrument User's Manual* provides precise information about what should be included in this item, and these definitions should be taken literally. According to the manual, current CMS policy regarding falls includes the following:

- An episode in which a resident lost his or her balance and would have fallen, were it not for staff intervention, is a fall. In other words, an intercepted fall is still a fall.

- The presence or absence of a resultant injury is not a factor in the definition of a fall. A fall without injury is still a fall.

- When a resident is found on the floor, the facility is obligated to investigate how he or she got there and put into place an intervention to prevent it from happening again. Unless there is evidence suggesting otherwise, the most logical conclusion is that a fall has occurred.

- The distance to the next lower surface (in this case, the floor) is not a factor in determining whether a fall occurred. If a resident rolled off a bed or mattress that was close to the floor, the incident is still a fall.

The point of accurately capturing occurrences of falls on the assessment is to identify and communicate resident problems and potential problems so staff will consider and use interventions to prevent falls and injuries from falls. If a resident rolls off a mattress that is close to the floor, it is still recorded as a fall, even if staff have already determined that placing a bed close to the floor to avoid injuries from falls is the best intervention for the resident (see the *Long Term Care Facility Resident Assessment Instrument User's Manual* p. 3-146 for supporting language).

Section O—Medications

The four areas that make up Section O, medications, are intended to capture different types of information; therefore, it is important to be familiar with the details of each's instructions. Coding errors are common in this section due to the following occurrences:

Miscounting the number of different medications used in the past seven days in item O1, number of medications

This item captures the number of different medications the resident actually received, and the *Long Term Care Facility Resident Assessment Instrument User's Manual* instructions for this item are very detailed. As the manual indicates, **do not** count the following in item O1:

- The number of doses given of the same medication
- Different dosages of the same medication
- The same medication by a different name
- Medications ordered but not administered

- Topical preparations used for preventative skin care (e.g., moisturizers and moisture barriers)
- Total parenteral nutrition solution
- Heparin included in saline solution to irrigate a heparin lock
- Nutritional supplements that contain a vitamin or vitamins as some of their ingredients (code this in item K5f, dietary supplement between meals)
- Herbal and alternative medicine products

On the other hand, **do** count the following for item O1:

- Over-the-counter and prescription drugs
- Medications administered by any route
- Routine doses administered
- Stat doses
- PRN (as needed) doses given
- Medications administered off-site while still a resident of the facility
- Self-administered medications
- Topical preparations, ointments, and creams used in wound care (e.g., Elase)
- Eye drops
- Vitamins
- Suppositories
- Antigens (e.g., PPD skin test for tuberculosis)
- Vaccines
- Medications added to total parenteral nutrition (e.g., electrolytes, vitamins, and insulin)

Here are other applicable rules for coding medications in item O1:

- Each type of insulin administered counts as a separate medication.
- A combination product counts as one medication.
- Long-acting medications (e.g., B12 and long-acting antipsychotics) administered prior to the observation period should be counted if they are still active during the observation period. To determine whether a medication is still active, consult a physician, a pharmacist, or the *Physician's Desk Reference* for input into the decision.

Miscounting the number of days injections were received in the past seven days for item O3, injections

All injections administered by any route—subcutaneous, intramuscular, or intradermal—are to be counted for this item. A common error is counting the number of injections given instead of the number of days during which injections were given. Also, antigens and vaccines are often erroneously left out of the count. When medication is administered by subcutaneous pump, count only the number of days on which the subcutaneous injection site was changed.

Coding medications incorrectly in item O4, days received the following medication

For the categories of medications listed on the MDS (i.e., antipsychotic, antianxiety, antidepressant, hypnotic, and diuretic), code according to the classification of the drug, not according to its use. For example, if the antidepressant trazodone is given for insomnia, code it as an antidepressant because that is its classification regardless of the reason for its use.

Section P—Special treatments and procedures

This section is subject to considerable scrutiny because of its significant role in SNF PPS reimbursement. Interestingly enough, studies have found that many errors occur related to failure to capture special treatments, procedures, and programs during the 14-day lookback period, which means that there is little evidence that providers are "gaming" the system.

With the 2006 implementation of the new rehabilitation plus extensive services RUG categories, accuracy in capturing care and services in P1a, special care treatments, and P1b, therapies, is more important than ever.

Item P1—Special treatments, procedures, and programs

If the items listed in P1a, special care treatments, occurred during the observation period, they are to be coded on the MDS regardless of where the services were delivered. In addition, these treatments are to be captured in the lookback period even when they occurred prior to admission, except in the circumstances outlined below. Special care programs under item P1a, however, are to be coded only if they were received within the nursing facility. Follow these important rules to avoid coding errors:

- Services provided solely in conjunction with a surgical or diagnostic procedure and the immediate postoperative or postprocedure recovery period are not to be coded on the MDS, per the *Long Term Care Facility Resident Assessment Instrument User's Manual, p. 3-182.*

- Item P1ac, IV medications; P1ak, transfusions; P1al, ventilator or respirator; and the other items in P1 can be captured in the lookback to the hospital according to the rules specified in the *Long Term Care Facility Resident Assessment Instrument User's Manual.* Under the administrative presumption of coverage, some of these services under some circumstances may be the only justification for covering a resident under Medicare Part A. However, when a surgical procedure was the only reason the service was provided, the service cannot be captured on the MDS. For example, IV medications administered prophylactically in the hospital in association with a total hip replacement would not be captured on the MDS. (However, if the medication order were continued upon admission to the SNF, it would be captured on the MDS.)

- IV medications administered in the hospital for a medical condition such as pneumonia would be captured on the MDS in the lookback period into the hospital, depending on the date selected for the assessment reference date.

- IV medications and blood transfusions provided during chemotherapy and dialysis are not captured on the MDS. IV fluids administered during these treatments are not coded on the MDS, either.

Item P1b—Therapies

Facility staff must maintain accurate treatment records to code item P1b, therapies, correctly. Errors in this section often are due to inaccurate documentation of treatment time. Although treatment logs are not specifically required for coding therapy minutes, their use is a standard clinical practice and expected of therapists.

Therapy minutes also must be documented in the clinical record, usually on a treatment grid. Information gleaned from these sources is used for coding item P1b. To ensure accuracy, the therapists' system for collecting treatment minutes must be consistent and reliable. In addition, it is important to routinely verify that the minutes were accurately transcribed from the treatment log to the treatment record in the chart and, in turn, onto the MDS.

Meticulous technique in calculating therapy minutes is critical to accuracy. Exact minutes must be entered for this item—it is not appropriate to calculate minutes from units in the way they are used for Part B billing, and it is not acceptable to round minutes up or down. Also, because computational errors are frequent, it is recommended that a calculator be used to total the minutes and that the addition be double-checked by a second person.

The rules regarding what therapy minutes to count in item P1b are specific. Only actual, medically necessary minutes of skilled therapy ordered by a physician and received by the resident after admission to the SNF can be counted. Within those parameters, the resident's time spent in therapy is counted. Therapy time starts when the resident begins the first treatment activity or task, although setup time is also counted. Therapy time ends when the resident finishes with the last apparatus and the treatment ends. Documentation time is not counted.

Following are additional tips for coding therapy on the MDS:

- Do not include time spent on the initial evaluation, but include time spent on periodic, medically necessary reevaluations during the course of ongoing treatment.
- Maintenance therapy is not counted once the program has been developed.
- Therapy that is not coverable as a skilled service and is paid for by the resident or family is not counted.
- Medically necessary therapy delivered at another location after admission to the SNF is counted as long as it was ordered by a physician and performed by a

licensed and qualified therapist. According to the PPS Final Rule, include the time it takes for the therapist to take the beneficiary to his or her home for a home visit before discharge, as long as the therapist uses the time in the car to teach or discuss the beneficiary's treatment or treatment goals. Also include family conferences for which the beneficiary is also present.

- Line-of-sight supervision by a licensed, qualified therapist is required to count therapy aide and therapy student minutes.

Those involved in the MDS process must calculate group therapy minutes accurately. Group therapy time for each discipline can be captured on the MDS only if some individual therapy has been delivered. Group therapy time that exceeds 25% of the total treatment time per discipline cannot be counted on the MDS. The calculation that determines the maximum number of group minutes permitted is a frequent source of error.

To calculate minutes for item P1b when group therapy has been delivered, follow these steps:

- Total the minutes of individual therapy delivered by the discipline
- Divide that total by three to find the maximum number of group therapy minutes that may be captured for that discipline
- Add the individual minutes delivered to the group minutes delivered (not to exceed the maximum group minutes calculated above) to find the allowable minutes for P1b for that discipline for that resident

Item P3—Nursing rehabilitation/restorative care

This section plays a significant role in reimbursement for the rehabilitation low RUG group and all of the nonskilled RUG groups. In addition, Medicare Part A coverage for skilled restorative care depends on this item.

To be coded in item P3, the activities listed in this section—items P3a through P3k—must meet all of the requirements listed on pp. 3-191–3-195 of the *Long Term Care Facility Resident Assessment Instrument User's Manual*. Some of the most common errors in this section are related to the following requirements:

- Measurable objectives and interventions must be documented in the care plan and in the clinical record.

- Evidence of periodic evaluation by a licensed nurse must be present in the clinical record.

- Nurse assistants and aides must be trained in the techniques that promote resident involvement in the activity.

- These activities must be carried out or supervised by members of the nursing staff. If the restorative nursing program is supervised by a rehabilitation therapist, it does not qualify for coding in this section. Rehabilitation therapists may carry out these activities, but in that case, the actions would be coded as nursing rehabilitation/restorative care in item P3 and would not be captured as therapy minutes in item P1b.

For any of these activities to contribute to a RUG category, they must be carried out for at least six days per week.

Item P4—Restraints

Studies indicate that this item still confounds some providers. Errors are common in coding restraints, partly because the instructions require a two-part decision-making process. The decision to code a device listed in item P4 as a restraint is based entirely on the effect the device has on the resident.

The items in P4, devices and restraints, include

- bed rails—full bed rails on all open sides of bed
- bed rails—other types of side rails used (e.g., half rail, one side)
- trunk restraint
- limb restraint
- chair prevents rising

Regardless of what the device is called (e.g., "postural support") or what the intended use is (e.g., for safety or to assist with positioning in bed), if it has the effect of restraining the resident as defined in the *Long Term Care Facility Resident Assessment Instrument User's Manual*, then it must be coded as a restraint. If the device does not restrain the resident, it must not be coded in item P4.

Therefore, the first part of the decision-making process is to answer whether the resident uses one of the devices listed in items P4a through P4e. If the answer is yes, then before item P4 can be coded, another question must be answered: Does the device meet this definition: "any manual method or physical or mechanical device, material, or equipment attached or adjacent to the resident's body that the individual cannot remove easily which restricts freedom of movement or normal access to one's body"? In other words, does the device prevent the resident from doing something functionally that he or she could otherwise do if the device were not in place?

For example, if a resident is not able to get out of bed unassisted, then siderails would not restrain him or her and would not be coded on the MDS. On the other hand, if the resident is able to get out of bed unassisted—even if he or she gets up and then falls down—and the siderails prevent him or her from doing this, then the siderails restrain the resident and must be coded in item P4. The same rule applies to the other items in P4.

It is important to note that the coding decision with regard to siderails in P4 is unrelated to the coding for item G6b, bed rails used for bed mobility or transfer. They are completely separate coding decisions.

Item P7—Physician visits

Physician visits and physician orders (item P8) are used in the RUG system as a bellwether for instability of a resident's status. Thus, inaccurate coding of these items can result in classifying a resident into a RUG category when he or she otherwise would not qualify for coverage. Consequently, it is important to understand the coding rules to avoid overcoding these items. On the other hand, Part A coverage might be denied to a resident inappropriately if these items are undercoded.

This item is intended to capture the number of days on which a physician examined the resident, not the number of visits by a physician. "Physician" is defined in the *Long Term Care Facility Resident Assessment Instrument User's Manual* as an MD, DO, podiatrist, or dentist who is either the primary physician or consultant; or an authorized physician assistant, nurse practitioner, or clinical nurse specialist working in collaboration with the physician.

Any physician examination other than an emergency department visit can be captured on the MDS as long as the beneficiary was a resident of the SNF at the time of the examination. Thus, the examination may have occurred at the facility or at the physician's office, or it may have occurred at another location, such as while the resident received dialysis or chemotherapy. The key is that the clinical record must reflect at least a partial examination by the physician, documented by the physician. It is not sufficient for a nurse to document that the physician examined the resident.

Item P8—Physician orders

This item is intended to capture the number of days on which a physician changed the resident's orders during the 14-day lookback period (or since admission, whichever is more recent), rather than the number of order changes. It focuses on orders for new or altered treatments after admission, including consultation orders. The definition of "physician" for this item is the same as the definition for item P7, physician visits. An order may be received by telephone or fax or written in person by the physician.

Coding errors for this item often are due to misunderstanding the types of orders that are acceptable to capture. To avoid overcoding this item, do not include:

- standard admission orders. However, orders written on the day of admission as a result of an unexpected change or deterioration should be counted.
- return admission orders.
- renewal orders that do not change the original orders.
- clarifying orders that do not change the original orders.
- sliding scale orders after the initial order for the sliding scale is captured.
- PRN orders after the initial order for the PRN medication is captured.
- orders written by a pharmacist.
- orders for transfer of care to another physician.

Section T—Therapy supplement for Medicare PPS

This section is required for all Medicare five-day and Medicare readmission/return assessments. (Note that individual states may have additional requirements for this section.) However, it is important to read the instructions for each item in the section because not all of the items are required for all assessments.

The readmission/return assessment is required when a resident who is covered by Part A is admitted to the hospital and returns to the nursing home covered by Part A. This assessment often erroneously omits Section T.

The other vulnerable areas of this section are items T1b, T1c, and T1d, where rehabilitation therapists must estimate the number of days and minutes of therapy the resident will receive through day 15 of the Medicare Part A stay. To avoid error, the following rules must be applied:

- Estimates of the number of therapy days and minutes in items T1c and T1d are not to be completed unless item T1b, ordered therapies, is coded "1," yes. This indicates that the physician has ordered at least one of the following services in the first 14 days of the Medicare Part A stay: physical therapy (PT), occupational therapy (OT), or speech pathology services.

- Items T1c and T1d should not be completed if the initial evaluation is completed but therapy treatments will not be scheduled.

- The estimate of the number of therapy days and minutes must include minutes already delivered and coded in item P1b, therapies.

- Calculate the expected number of days or minutes through day 15, even if the resident is discharged prior to day 15.

- The number of days in T1c should reflect the actual number of calendar days that at least one therapy service will be provided. For example, if PT is provided on Monday, Wednesday, and Friday and OT is provided on the same days, T1c would be coded as three days.

- If the physician orders therapy for 10 days, the projected number of days in Section T will be 10—assuming that therapy is provided five days per week—rather than 14. Likewise, if the physician does not order a limited number of days, the projection will be based on the entire two weeks, assuming that the beneficiary continues to stay and receive services.

- If the physician orders therapy for a limited number of days, then the projection must be for that number of days. For example, if therapy is ordered for five days, then the number if days in item T1c will be "5."

- Do not include therapy evaluation minutes in the estimate of minutes.

- Do not count the evaluation day in the estimate of days unless treatment is rendered.

The MDS and the nine new RUG categories

In January 2006, CMS implemented nine new RUG categories, combining the already existing rehabilitation categories and extensive services category. These RUG refinements were an effort to better reimburse SNF providers for Medicare Part A residents receiving both skilled rehabilitation services and extensive skilled nursing services (e.g., parenteral/IV, IV medication, suctioning, tracheostomy care, ventilator, or respirator).

Prior to implementation of this 53-RUG system, providers aimed to classify residents into the rehabilitation RUGs to obtain the best reimbursement—even when the resident also received extensive skilled nursing services. Because the new categories now offer the best reimbursement for these complex residents who receive both types of skilled care, providers must refocus attention on

- efforts to determine which, if any, of the treatments in MDS section P1a, special care treatments, the resident received in the hospital.

- obtaining documentation from the hospital that the services were delivered and the last date on which they were delivered.

- determining the best date for setting the ARD in order to capture the reimbursement that will pay them most accurately for the services provided. In some cases, a resident may classify into a rehabilitation RUG, a clinical RUG, and the combined rehabilitation plus extensive services RUG, depending on where the ARD is set.

Common MDS-related errors that affect the claim

This book has already discussed some of the obvious errors that affect billing (e.g., incorrect therapy minutes or physician visits, which would result in an incorrect RUG level), but there are others. Fiscal intermediaries (FI) and government agencies monitoring the accuracy of Medicare Part A bills have identified several other common errors, such as the following:

Inconsistent ARDs among disciplines

As indicated earlier in the discussion of Section G1, the ARD establishes the end of the observation period for all MDS items. When all interdisciplinary team members do not use the same ARD, different observation periods are used for the same assessment. The result is that some care and services are inappropriately captured on the MDS and billed to Medicare or Medicaid.

Failure to capture off-cycle assessments, resulting in inappropriate RUG payments

Off-cycle assessments are SNF PPS assessments that are required by government regulations but fall outside of the regular schedule of assessments.

The Other Medicare Required Assessment (OMRA) is designed to calculate a nonrehabilitation RUG level eight to 10 days after all rehabilitation has been discontinued when the resident continues to receive a skilled service. Failure to complete or bill for the OMRA can result in higher reimbursement than the facility is entitled to and possible accusations of Medicare fraud or abuse. On the other hand, failure to complete or to bill for OMRAs might mean that a facility is missing legitimate opportunities for continued Part A coverage if residents are discontinued from skilled coverage when therapy ends—even when skilled care continues in the form of nursing care.

Significant Change in Status Assessments (SCSA) reflect the requirement for clinical reassessment if the resident's status meets specific criteria listed in Chapter 2 of the *Long Term Care Facility Resident Assessment Instrument User's Manual.*

The Medicare-required assessments listed in MDS item AA8a calculate RUG categories, but the SCSA is the only clinical assessment from item AA8a that has the potential to change the RUG category.

If SCSAs are not completed, clinical staff may not be identifying status changes in their residents, and the quality of care may suffer as a result.

In addition, when a SCSA is performed on a SNF PPS resident outside of the window of a regularly scheduled PPS assessment (the five-day, 14-day, 30-day assessments, etc.), it is important to verify that the assessment was coded on the MDS as an OMRA in addition to being coded as a SCSA. Although this assessment is not an OMRA and the OMRA criteria do not apply in this case, this coding is mandated by CMS to update the RUG calculation. Failure to code properly could result in suspicions of fraud or abuse or, alternatively, could result in lower RUG levels than the facility is entitled to.

In addition, errors also occur when facility staff are not clear about when the RUG level changes for off-cycle assessments. For the OMRA and SCSA, the RUG level changes on the ARD of the off-cycle assessment unless the ARD falls within the grace days of a regularly scheduled assessment. In that case, the RUG level changes on the first day of the regular payment block.

Service dates that do not match the ARD

The service date on the claim form is the ARD from the MDS. Facility operational systems must ensure clear communication from the clinical team to the billing office to ensure that information about all PPS MDSs is communicated completely and accurately.

Incorrect Health Insurance PPS (HIPPS) codes

Each PPS assessment in the billing period must be represented by a five-position code indicating the RUG level and the type of assessment. HIPPS code errors, which are due to either an incorrect RUG level or incorrect assessment type, often occur when lines of communication between the clinical team and billing office are not optimal.

Failure to account for leave-of-absence days

Leave-of-absence (LOA) days are not counted in the PPS assessment schedule. For example, a resident was admitted on November 7, so the ARD for the five-day assessment was required to be any day from November 7 to November 14 (days one through eight of the Medicare stay). However, the resident spent a few hours in the emergency room of the acute hospital in that time, including one midnight. Consequently, that day is not counted when determining the window for setting the ARD. The new window would be November 7 to November 15.

Billing errors also sometimes result from a poor understanding of the time period covered by a particular MDS assessment. For example, the five-day PPS MDS pays for days one through 14 of the Medicare Part A stay, the 14-day assessment covers days 15–30, and so on.

When a Medicare Part A resident is out of the facility at midnight and not formally discharged from the facility, it is considered a leave of absence, and the provider is not permitted to bill for the day prior to the midnight absence. If lines of communication are not effective in informing the billing office of these absences, the billers will not know to exclude those days from the bill. As a result, the facility may receive Medicare money to which it is not entitled, and the days will be inappropriately deducted from the resident's 100-day SNF benefit period.

Summary

The complexity of the coding rules and the related need for attention to detail dictate that individuals completing the MDS must demonstrate the expertise needed to achieve accuracy. Intimate familiarity with the *Long Term Care Facility Resident Assessment Instrument User's Manual* is the number one prerequisite for achieving MDS coding accuracy. In addition, because the rules and regulations are subject to frequent updating, it is critical to ensure that MDS assessors have access to the most current version of the manual.

Updates are posted both on the CMS Web site at *www.cms.hhs.gov/NursingHomeQualityInits/* and on the HCPro Web Site at *www.hcpro.com/long-term-care/* by clicking on "MDS/PPS" under the Long-Term Care Information Center at the bottom left of the page.

Chapter 2

THE AUDITS

Traditionally, long-term care providers have focused their efforts on chasing after negative results. They typically follow up after a poor survey or investigate unfavorable QI/QMs and QMs or an unexpected change in RUG trends after they've already tried to determine what went wrong.

It is more productive to conduct auditing activities on a concurrent basis to identify and correct problems before they become trends—and before they become significant problems for residents or for the facility. In conjunction with concurrent audits, however, retrospective review—looking back after the fact—can be useful in looking at the overall picture of facility performance.

The goals of retrospective audits focused on MDS accuracy are as follows:

1. To validate that staff members coding the MDS are using current coding instructions, found in the *Long Term Care Facility Resident Assessment Instrument User's Manual*

2. To validate that timing and scheduling requirements are met

3. To verify that the appropriate lookback periods are used for each item

4. To verify that the clinical record supports the coding entered on the MDS

5. To ensure that data used to make coding decisions is collected from all disciplines and sources and all shifts for the entire observation period

6. To confirm that MDS coding decisions are based on interviews with the resident (when possible); reports from staff members working with the resident, family members, and significant others; and on record review and direct observation by the assessor

7. To determine whether any discrepancies found in the supporting documentation are resolved and whether the coding decision is accurate

The goals of audits focused on SNF PPS reimbursement center on MDS accuracy, as indicated above, and include the following:

1. To verify technical eligibility for Part A coverage

2. To confirm that MDS information on the UB-92 form is accurate

3. To determine whether off-cycle assessments are captured on the claim form

4. To verify accuracy of HIPPS codes on the claim form

5. To validate that the RUG levels are consistent with rehabilitation therapy ancillaries on the claim form

6. To corroborate the accuracy of the therapy minutes that underlie the rehabilitation RUG categories billed

7. To verify service captured in the lookback into the hospital stay

8. To confirm that MDS assessments are transmitted prior to billing

Content of audits

Documentation to support MDS coding

Auditing can be accomplished by several different methods, as discussed further in this chapter. Despite differences in audits and despite the fact that each item has its own unique coding rules, however, audits for most MDS items have one thing in common: the search for clinical record documentation to corroborate the coding decisions. Consequently, the auditor must understand clearly what to look for in the medical record.

For example, if the chart reflects "agitation" by the resident, it is not appropriate for the assessor to independently translate that "agitation" into a specific behavior for item E4, behavior symptoms, unless the actual behavior is specified in the record. Documentation by clinical staff who witnessed the behavior should indicate the specific conduct, such as hitting staff, screaming, wandering aimlessly into another's room, etc.

Another case is item I1i, hallucinations. For this item, it is not sufficient to document that the resident was hallucinating. Chart documentation should include a description of the auditory, visual, tactile, olfactory, or gustatory false perceptions that occurred in the absence of real stimuli.

The documentation guide on the following pages provides suggestions for the kind of supporting documentation that may be appropriate for the 108 MDS items used to calculate the RUGs. See Figure 2.1.

Once the assessor is familiar with the kind of information needed to support the MDS items, it may be helpful to use a form to document audit findings. See Figure 2.2 for an MDS documentation review form.

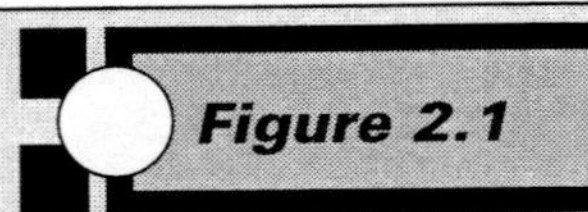

Figure 2.1 MDS documentation guide for PPS

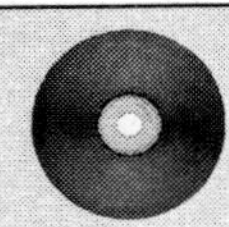

Location key:

Act --------	Activities	MDN -------	M.D. notes	RD -------	Dietician	SS ------	Social Services
CNA-------	Nursing Assistant	NN -------	Nurses notes	Rehab -----	Therapy notes	Tx -------	Treatment sheets
MAR-------	Medication record	RCP -------	Care plan	RNA -----	Restorative	POS------	Physicians order sheet

MDS Section	Suggested Supporting Documentation	Possible Location of Documentation
B. Cognitive Patterns		
1.Comatose	Specific diagnosis from physician of coma or persistent vegetative state and condition meets description in *RAI User's Manual.*	POS, MDN, NN, RCP
2.Short-term memory	Specific examples of short-term memory problems, such as unable to describe an activity just completed after five minutes.	MDN, NN, SS, Act, Rehab, CNA, RNA, RCP
4.Daily decision-making	Examples of resident's ability or inability re: decision-making, such as unable to decide which blouse to wear.	NN, SS, Act, Rehab, CNA, RNA, RCP
C. Communication/Hearing Patterns		
4.Making self understood	Examples of word-finding problems or difficulty expressing thoughts; verbalizations limited to concrete requests only.	MDN, NN, SS, Act, Rehab, CNA, RNA, RCP, RD
E. Mood and Behavior Patterns		
1.Depressed, anxious, sad –Verbal expressions of distress	Examples of verbal and/or non-verbal expressions of distress as detailed on the MDS, such as specific negative statements, repetitive questions, complaint verbalizations, persistent anger.	MDN, NN, SS, Act, Rehab, CNA, RNA, RCP, RD
–Sleep-cycle issues	Specific descriptions of unpleasant mood in the morning and/or specifics of insomnia or change in usual sleep pattern.	NN, SS, Act, Rehab, CNA, RNA, RCP
–Sad, apathetic, anxious appearance	Specific details of facial expressions, crying, repetitive physical movements.	NN, SS, Act, Rehab, CNA, RNA, RCP
–Loss of interest	Examples of withdrawal from activities and/or reduced social interaction.	NN, SS, Act, Rehab, CNA, RNA, RCP
4.Behavioral symptoms	Details of incidents of behavior symptoms and patterns, such as hitting staff, screaming, wandering aimlessly into another's room.	NN, SS, Act, CNA, RCP
G. Physical Functioning and Structural Problems		
1.Bed mobility, transfer, eating, toilet use	The resident's self-performance and support provided must reflect performance across all shifts/all disciplines for all ADLs.	NN, Rehab, CNA, RNA, RCP
H. Continence in Last 14 Days		
3. Appliances and programs	Chart must reflect implementation of a plan for scheduled toileting, such as taking resident to the bathroom or bedside commode, or offering the urinal; and/or a formal bladder retraining program.	NN, CNA, RNA, RCP, POS
I. Disease Diagnoses		
1. Diabetes Mellitus, aphasia, Cerebral Palsy, Hemiplegia/ Hemipareis, MS, Quadraplegia	For each diagnosis checked, the chart must show ACTIVE physician diagnoses that have relationships to CURRENT ADL, cognitive, or mood/ behavior status; medical treatments; nursing monitoring; or risk of death. Signs/symptoms and/or monitoring for signs/symptoms should be evident.	POS, MDN, NN, RCP, MAR Lab
2. Infections: Pneumonia, Septicemia	As above. In addition, pertinent lab work, chest x-ray, medication orders, and assessment of fever and signs/symptoms.	POS, MDN, NN, RCP, MAR Lab, X-ray
J. Health Conditions		
1c. Dehydrated; output greater then imput	Intake & output assessments; nursing assessments of physical status, signs/symptoms, fluid loss; lab results.	NN, RCP, Lab
1e. Delusions	Description of resident's fixed, false beliefs, not shared by others, even when there is proof or evidence to the contrary.	NN, SS, Act, CNA, RCP
1h. Fever	Record of temperature 2.4 degrees > baseline using same route of temp measurement each time. Signs/symptoms of fever.	NN, vital signs sheet
1i. Hallucinations	Description of auditory, visual, tactile, olfactory, or gustatory false perceptions that occur in the absence of real stimuli.	POS, MDN, NN, SS, MAR, RCP
1j. Internal bleeding	Clinical evidence such as coffee ground emesis; black, tarry stools; hematuria; hemoptysis. Physical & vital signs assessments.	MDN, NN, vital signs sheet, RCP

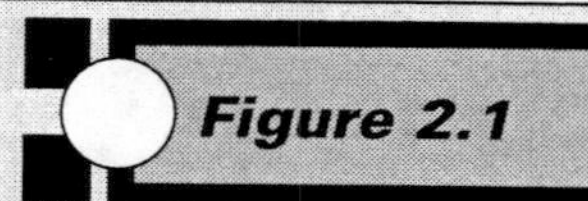

Figure 2.1 MDS documentation guide for PPS (cont.)

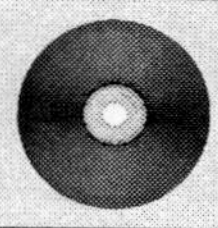

MDS Section	Suggested Supporting Documentation	Possible Location of Documentation
1o. Vomiting	Detail of each incident.	POS, NN, RCP
K. Oral/Nutritional Status		
3. Weight loss	Record of weight loss as defined on the MDS. Include analysis of weight trend, appetite, lab results.	POS, MDN, NN, SS, RD, weight record, RCP
5a. Parenteral/IV	Evidence of IV therapy during the reference period.	Hospital record, POS, NN, IV flowsheet, RCP
b. Tube feeding	Evidence of tube feeding accounting for at least 51% of daily calories OR at least 26% of daily calories and 501cc daily intake.	POS, NN, I & O sheet, RD, RCP
6a. IV/tubefeeding calories	Record of proportion of calories received through parenteral or tube feedings during the reference period.	POS, NN, I & O sheet, RD, RCP
b. IV/TF fluid intake	Record of average fluid intake per day by IV or tubefeeding.	POS, NN, I & O sheet, RD, RCP
M. Skin Condition		
1 & 2. Ulcers	Assessment and documentation of ulcers as defined in manual. For M1, only ulcers due to circulation, pressure, and other diseases.	Admission notes, NN, POS, tx sheets, skin sheets, RCP
4. Burns, open lesions other than ulcers, rashes, cuts; surgical wounds.	Documentation of assessment of these conditions, including appearance measurements, treatments, color, odor. Includes healing and non-healing open or closed surgical incisions, skin grafts, or drainage sites.	Admission notes, NN, POS, tx sheets, skin sheets, MDN, RCP
5. Skin treatments	Evidence of consistent use of devices, dressings, treatments, programs for prevention and treatment of skin problems.	POS, NN, tx sheets, skin sheets, CNA, RCP
6. –Infection of the foot –Open foot lesions –Dressings to foot	Documentation of assessment of these conditions, including appearance, measurements, treatments, color, odor. Includes evidence of dressing changes.	POS, MDN, NN, tx sheets, MAR, RCP, skin sheets
N. Activity Pursuit Patterns		
1. Time awake	Record of resident's sleep/nap habits in morning, afternoon, and evening.	NN, CAN, Act, SS, RCP
O. Medications		
3. Injections	Details of type, frequency, effectiveness of injections.	POS, NN, MAR, diabetic/ anticoagulant flow sheet
P. Special Treatments and Procedures		
1a. Special care: chemotherapy, dialysis, IV meds, O_2 therapy, radiation, suctioning, trach care, transfusions, ventilator or respirator	Evidence of any of these treatments or procedures must be detailed in the medical record. They may be received by the resident either at the facility or as a hospital outpatient or inpatient during the assessment period to be included on the MDS. Do not include services provided in conjunction with a surgical procedure, unless such a service is continued at the SNF.	Hospital records, NN, tx sheets, MARs, POS, MDN, H&P, discharge summary, RCP
b. Therapies: Speech, OT, PT, RT	Total number of days each therapy was administered for at least 15 minutes per day, and the total number of minutes provided during the assessment period must be detailed in the chart. COUNT POST-ADMISSION THERAPIES ONLY. Do NOT look back into hospital stay.	Daily time sheets, daily treatment sheets, POS, RCP: CROSS-CHECK WITH THERAPY LOGS & UB-92
3. Nursing rehab/Restorative care	Daily record of each restorative/rehab nursing treatment. Must meet the *RAI User's Manual* definitions.	POS, NN, RNA, RCP
7. Physician visits	Physician documentation of an examination must be in the chart. Visit may occur off-site after SNF admission (except emergency room).	POS, MDN, NN
8. Physician orders	Includes written, telephone, fax, or consultation orders for new or changed treatment. Does NOT include admission or renewal orders without changes.	POS, NN, MDN
T. Therapy Supplement for Medicare PPS		
1. Special treatments and procedures	Details of therapy ordered to begin within first 14 days of stay.	POS, MDN, NN, Rehab

Source: Rena R. Shephard, RRS Healthcare Consulting Services. Used with permission.

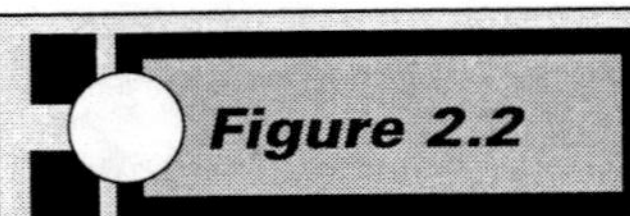

Figure 2.2 MDS documentation review

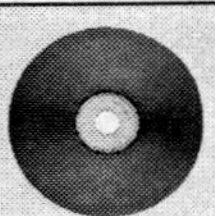

INSTRUCTIONS: For each section:

1. Place a check mark next to the appropriate response for this resident in the Resident Data column.
2. In the next column, identify the location(s) in the chart where the supporting documentation is located and the date(s) of the entries.
3. Discrepancies in the supporting documentation may be appropriate under some circumstances. Where discrepancies exist, mark in the next column if they have been reconciled. **
4. In the next column, identify the date the item was completed on this form.
5. Place your initials in the Initials column.

All discrepancies must be brought to the attention of the Director of Nursing and the Interdisciplinary Team

MDS Item		Reference Window	Resident data	Date and Location of Supporting Documentation	Discrepancies Reconciled Yes	Discrepancies Reconciled No	Date
B. Cognitive Patterns		7 days					
Comatose	No						
	Yes						
Short-term Memory	Memory OK						
	Memory problem						
Cognitive Skills for Daily Decision-Making	Independent						
	Modified independent						
C. Communication		7 days					
Making Self Understood	Understood						
	Usually understood						
	Sometimes understood						
	Rarely/Never understood						
E. Mood and Behavior		30 days					
Indicators of Depression, Anxiety, Sad Mood	Verbal expressions of distress						
	Made negative statements						
	Repetitive questions						
	Repetitive verbalizations						
	Persistent anger with self or others						
	Self deprecation						
	Expressions of what appear to be unrealistic fears						
	Recurrent statements something terrible is about to happen						
	Repetitive health complaints						
	Repetitive anxious complaints/concerns (non-health related)						
	Sleep-cycle issues						
	Unpleasant mood in morning						
	Insomnia/change in usual sleep pattern						

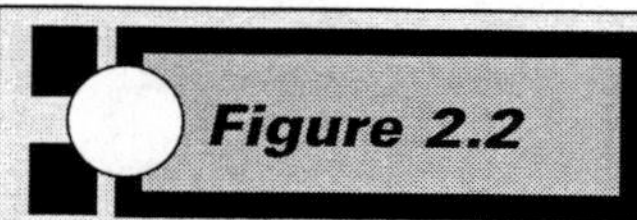

MDS documentation review (cont.)

MDS Item		Reference Window	Resident data	Date and Location of Supporting Documentation	Discrepancies Reconciled Yes	Discrepancies Reconciled No	Date
Indicators of Depression, Anxiety, Sad Mood (continued)	Sad, apathetic, anxious appearance	30 days					
	Sad, pained, worried facial expression						
	Crying, tearfulness						
	Repetitive physical movements						
	Loss of interest						
	Withdrawal from activities of interest						
	Reduced social interaction						
Behavioral Symptoms - Frequency		7 days					
Wandering	Not exhibited in last 7 days						
	Occurred 1 to 3 days in last 7						
	Occurred 4 to 6 days but < daily						
	Occurred daily						
Verbally abusive behavioral symptoms	Not exhibited in last 7 days						
	Occurred 1 to 3 days in last 7						
	Occurred 4 to 6 days but < daily						
	Occurred daily						
Physically abusive behavioral symptoms	Not exhibited in last 7 days						
	Occurred 1 to 3 days in last 7						
	Occurred 4 to 6 days but < daily						
	Occurred daily						
Socially inappropriate/ disruptive behavioral symptoms	Not exhibited in last 7 days						
	Occurred 1 to 3 days in last 7						
	Occurred 4-6 days but < daily						
	Occurred daily						
Resists care	Not exhibited in last 7 days						
	Occurred 1 to 3 days in last 7						
	Occurred 4 to 6 days but < daily						
	Occurred daily						
Behavioral Symptoms - Alterability		7 days					
Wandering	Not present or easily altered						
	Not easily altered						

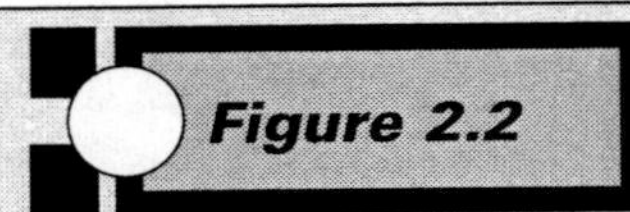

MDS documentation review (cont.)

MDS Item		Reference Window	Resident data	Date and Location of Supporting Documentation	Discrepancies Reconciled		Date
					Yes	No	
Verbally abusive behavioral symptoms	Not present or easily altered	7 days					
	Not easily altered						
Physically abusive behavioral symptoms	Not present or easily altered						
	Not easily altered						
Socially inappropriate/ disruptive	Not present or easily altered						
	Not easily altered						
Resists care	Not present or easily altered						
	Not easily altered						
G (A). Physical Functioning & Structural Problems ADL Self-performance		7 days					
Bed mobility	Independent						
	Supervision						
	Limited assistance						
	Extensive assistance						
	Total dependence						
	Activity did not occur						
Transfer	Independent						
	Supervision						
	Limited assistance						
	Extensive assistance						
	Total dependence						
	Activity did not occur						
Eating	Independent						
	Supervision						
	Limited assistance						
	Extensive assistance						
	Total dependence						
	Activity did not occur						
Toilet use	Independent						
	Supervision						
	Limited assistance						
	Extensive assistance						
	Total dependence						

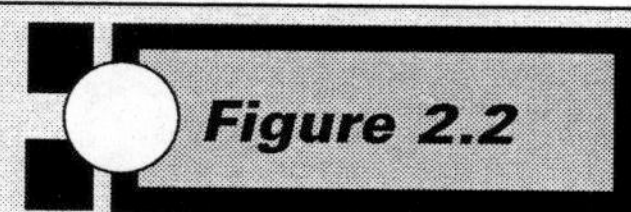

MDS documentation review (cont.)

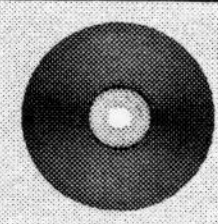

MDS Item		Reference Window	Resident data	Date and Location of Supporting Documentation	Discrepancies Reconciled		Date
					Yes	No	
Toilet use (continued)	Activity did not occur						
G(B). Physical Functioning & Structural Problems ADL Support Provided		7 days					
Bed mobility	No setup or physical help						
	Setup help only						
	One person physical assist						
	Two+ person physical assist						
	Activity did not occur at all						
Transfer	No setup or physical help						
	Setup help only						
	One person physical assist						
	Two+ person physical assist						
	Activity did not occur at all						
Eating	No setup or physical help						
	Setup help only						
	One person physical assist						
	Two+ person physical assist						
	Activity did not occur at all						
Toilet use	No setup or physical help						
	Setup help only						
	One person physical assist						
	Two+ person physical assist						
	Activity did not occur at all						
H. Continence		14 days					
Appliances and programs	Scheduled toileting program						
	Bladder retraining program						
I. Disease Diagnoses		Current diagnoses only					
Diseases	Diabetes Mellitus						
	Aphasia						
	Cerebral Palsy						
	Hemiplegia/Hemiparesis						
	Multiple Sclerosis						

MDS documentation review (cont.)

MDS Item		Reference Window	Resident data	Date and Location of Supporting Documentation	Discrepancies Reconciled		Date
					Yes	No	
Infections	Pneumonia						
	Septicemia						
J. Health Conditions		7 days					
Problem conditions	Dehydrated: Output > input						
	Delusions						
	Fever						
	Hallucinations						
	Internal bleeding						
	Vomiting						
K. Oral/Nutritional Status							
Weight change	Weight loss	30/180 days					
Nutritional approaches *✓UB-92]	Parenteral/IV	7 days					
	Feeding tube						
Parenteral or enteral intake Total calories [UB-92]	None						
	1% to 25%						
	26% to 50%						
	51% to 75%						
	76% to 100%						
Parenteral or enteral intake Fluid intake [UB-92]	None	7 days					
	1 to 500 cc/day						
	501 to 1,000 cc/day						
	1,001 to 1,500 cc/day						
	1,501 to 2,000 cc/day						
	2,001 or more cc/day						
M. Skin Conditions		7 days					
Ulcers [UB-92]	None						
	Stage 1						
	Stage 2						
	Stage 3						
	Stage 4						

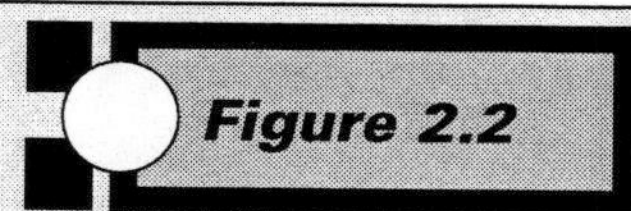

MDS documentation review (cont.)

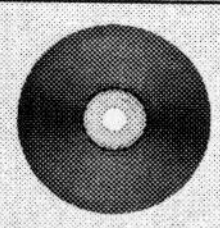

MDS Item		Reference Window	Resident data	Date and Location of Supporting Documentation	Discrepancies Reconciled Yes	Discrepancies Reconciled No	Date
					Yes	No	
Type of ulcer	Pressure ulcer	7 days					
Other skin problems or lesions present	None						
	Burns (2nd or 3rd degree)						
[UB-92]	Open lesions other than ulcers, rashes, cuts						
	Surgical wounds						
Skin treatments	None						
	Pressure relieving devices for chair						
[UB-92]	Pressure relieving devices for bed						
	Turning/repositioning program						
	Nutrition or hydration intervention for skin problems						
	Ulcer care						
	Surgical wound care						
	Application of dressings other than to feet						
	Application of ointments/meds other than to feet						
Foot problems and care	None						
	Infections of the foot–e.g., cellulitis, purulent drainage						
[UB-92]	Open lesions on the foot						
	Application of dressings						
N. Activity Pursuit Patterns							
Time awake: *all or most of the time*	Morning						
	Afternoon						
	Evening						
	None						
O. Medications							
Injections	No						
[UB-92]	Yes						

UB-92 claim form accuracy

MDS coding accuracy is critical to all MDS audits. However, audits for SNF PPS reimbursement contain additional tasks, one of which is verifying that the UB-92 claim form contains accurate information relative to the MDS data that must appear on the form. In addition, it is important to verify that the MDS was transmitted prior to billing. The only authoritative source for this information is the Final Validation Report generated by the state MDS database.

See the sample MDS/UB-92 audit tool in Figure 2.3 for details about these audits.

Auditing for daily skilled services for SNF PPS

In order to qualify for Part A reimbursement, the clinical record must demonstrate that a daily skilled service under Medicare definitions was provided. Monitor MDS information against the chart to ensure that the care and services provided are represented on the form and to ensure that the services are not overstated.

The MDS does not provide information about how often services were provided or during what period of time. Therefore, the clinical record must be audited to ensure that it supports the RUG level billed and verifies that a daily skilled service was provided. In addition, the audit should include verification that other relevant regulatory requirements have been met, such as the requirement for physician certification and recertification of the skilled need, the need for signed physician orders prior to billing, and the need for an MDS to be accepted into the state database prior to billing.

Some samples of these types of audit forms appear in Figures 2.4, 2.5, 2.6, and 2.7.

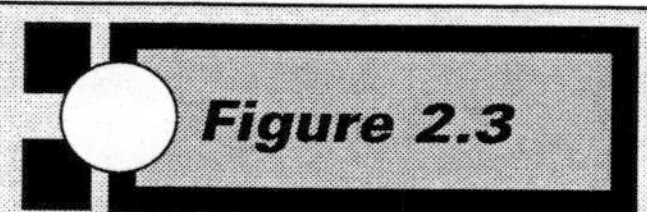

Figure 2.3 MDS/UB-92 audit tool

Technical eligibility

Requirement	Met	Not met	Comments
1. Medicare enrollment verified			
2. Medicare Secondary Payer Questionnaire completed			
3. Has benefits available			
–Common Working File checked			
–Prior stay form completed			
4. HMO membership ruled out			
5. 3-day qualifying hospital stay dates: ________________			
6. 30-day transfer requirement			
7. Covered condition is related to hospital stay or subsequent SNF stay			
8. Resident placed in certified bed			
9. Physician certification/recertification completed per regulation			
–Completed timely			
–Signed by authorized physician, NP, or CNS			
–Contains required content			
10. Orders signed prior to claim submission & implemented per orders			

MDS/UB-92 consistency

Data description	MDS data	UB-92 response	Comments
1. # of covered days @ FL7 = total accommodation units in FL47 (LOA days & day of d/c or death in FL8 are excluded)	N/A	FL7 / FL47	
2. HIPPS code relationship to assessment period	*ARD and service date must match*		
–HIPPS code #1	ARD:	Service date:	
–HIPPS code #2	ARD:	Service date:	
–HIPPS code #3	ARD:	Service date:	
3. HIPPS code relationship to RUG	*RUGs must match*		
–HIPPS code #1			
–HIPPS code #2			
–HIPPS code #3			
4. HIPPS code relationship to assessment type	*MDS & UB do not have to match but must not conflict*		
–HIPPS code #1			
–HIPPS code #2			
–HIPPS code #3			
5. HIPPS code relationship to therapy ancillaries (FL42)	*RUA, RUB, RUC need ≥ 2; other rehab RUGs need ≥ 1*		
–HIPPS code #1			
–HIPPS code #2			
–HIPPS code #3			
6. Number of assessments in claim period		#HIPPS codes	

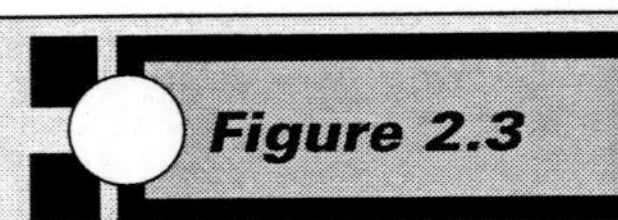

MDS/UB-92 audit tool (cont.)

Data description		MDS data	UB-92 response	Comments
7. Accuracy of off-cycle coverage dates (FL45 & 46)		*New RUG begins on ARD unless ARD falls within grace days, in which case the RUG begins day 1 of regular payment block; RUG continues until end of block or new assessment*		
–Assessment # 1	# covered days ——— →			
–Assessment #2	# covered days: ——— →			
–Assessment #3	# covered days: ——— →			
8. Therapy minutes/days relationship to RUG		MDS / Log	RUG	PT: OT: ST:
9. Line item charges reflected on MDS				
10. Principle diagnosis				
11. Diagnosis sequencing supports skilled need				
12. # MDS corrections / # adjustment bills				
13. Revenue code 0022 for each billed assessment		N/A		

MDS timing and scheduling

Requirement	Met	Not met	Comments
1. ARD set within required parameters for all MDSs in claim period			
2. AA9 signatures (IDT completion of sections) are on or after ARD			
3. R2b/VB2 dates (assessment coordinator) on or after last AA9 date			
4. R2b/VB2 dates no more than 14 days after ARD			
5. VB4 date (care plan completion) no more than 7 days after VB2			
6. Initial admission assessment completed (Vb2) no later than day 14			
7. OMRA: ARD day 8 to 10 after all therapy d/c'd if remained skilled			
8. Transmitted no > 31 days after R2b (Medicare) or VB4 (OBRA)			
9. Use of grace days is appropriate			
10. Validation reports indicate MDSs transmitted prior to billing			

Action plan

Deficiency	Action plan	By date	Person responsible

Source: Rena R. Shephard, RRS Healthcare Consulting Services. Used with permission.

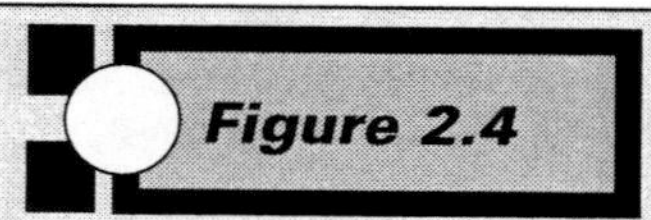

Med-A MDS/UB-92 audit

Resident Name or MR#: ____________________
Claim Period/Dates of Coverage: ____________________

TECHNICAL ELIGIBILITY	MET	NOT MET	N/A	COMMENTS
3 Day acute care stay (hospital or acute rehab)				
30 Day transfer				
Resident placed in certified bed				
Medicare enrollment verified				
Has Medicare benefits available				
Covered condition is related to hospital stay or subsequent SNF stay				
Physician certification/recertification:				
--Completed within acceptable time frame				
--Signed by authorized physician, NP or CNS				
--Contains required content				
Physician orders signed prior to claim submission				

ADL SCORE VERIFICATION
Verify score during reference period

ADL Activity Reviewed	MDS Score for Self-Performance	Chart Review Self-Performance Score	MDS Score for Staff Support	Chart Review Staff Support Score
Bed Mobility				
Transferring				
Toileting				
Eating				

Comments: ____________________

THERAPY VERIFICATION Verify minutes during reference period	MET	NOT MET	N/A	COMMENTS
SPEECH THERAPY: Actual treatment minutes entered on logs match minutes on Section P of the MDS				
PHYSICAL THERAPY: Actual treatment minutes entered on logs match minutes on Section P of the MDS				
OCCUPATIONAL THERAPY: Actual treatment minutes entered on logs match minutes on Section P of the MDS				
Therapy services were reasonable and necessary				
Therapy Plan of Care was signed by physician				

Total Therapy Days on Section P of the MDS:	Total Therapy Days After Audit of Record:	Total Therapy Minutes on Section P of the MDS:	Total Therapy Minutes After Audit of Record:

Comments: ____________________

____

Courtesy of Pam Manion, RN, MS, GCNS and the MU MDS and Quality Research Team, 2002.

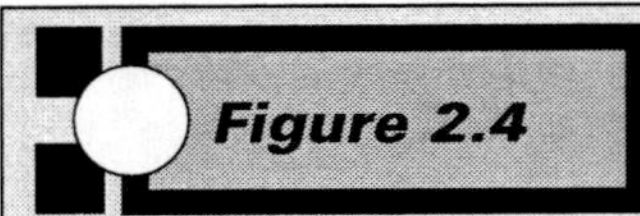

Med-A MDS/UB-92 audit (cont.)

Resident Name or MR#: ____________________

NON-REHAB RUG VERIFICATION	MET	NOT MET	N/A	COMMENTS
Services affecting RUG category are skilled, reasonable and necessary				
Documentation in record substantiates MDS scoring				

Comments: ____________________

RUG CLASS VERIFICATION	MET	NOT MET	N/A	COMMENTS
Identified RUGs category was correct based on record review				

Comments: ____________________

MDS TIMING & SCHEDULING	MET	NOT MET	N/A	COMMENTS
Correct reason for assessment				
ARD set w/in required parameters				
AA9 signatures (IDT completion) are on/after ARD				
Initial admission assessment (Vb2) not later than day 14				
For all assessments except admission, R2b/Vb2 dates no more than 14 days after ARD				
Vb4 date (care plan complete) no > than 7 days after Vb2				
R2b/Vb2 dates on/after last AA9 date				
For OMRA, ARD day 8-10 after all therapy DC'd if still skilled				
Transmitted no > 31 days after R2b/Vb4				
Use of grace days is appropriate				
Assessment accepted into state database prior to billing verified by validation report				

Comments: ____________________

BILLING UB-92 CLAIM	MET	NOT MET	N/A	COMMENTS
Statement period consistent with MDS				
Admission date correct				
ARD consistent with MDS ARD				
HIPPS code matches MDS reason for assessment				
Diagnoses match medical record and MDS				
Principle diagnosis is related to hospital stay and primary condition warranting Medicare coverage				
Secondary diagnoses relate to Medicare coverage or services billed				

Comments: ____________________

____

____

____

Courtesy of Pam Manion, RN, MS, GCNS and the MU MDS and Quality Research Team, 2002.

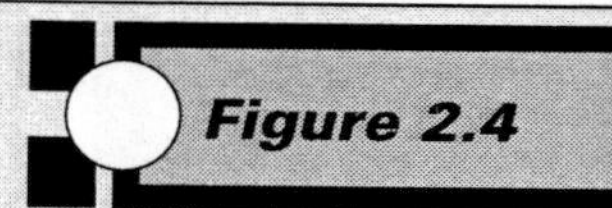

Figure 2.4 Med-A MDS/UB-92 audit (cont.)

Resident Name or MR#: ____________

ACTION PLAN

Problem Area	Plan to Correct	Projected Date	Person Responsible

Signatures and Titles of Reviewers : ______________________________
____
____
____

Date Review Completed: _________

REFERENCE INFORMATION

Physician Certification/Recertification Forms:

- ❑ Initial certification must be signed and dated at time of admission
- ❑ Re-certification must be signed and dated on or before day 14
- ❑ Following re-certifications must be signed and dated at intervals not exceeding 30 days

Medicare Assessment Schedule:

- ❑ 5 Day PPS Assessment – ARD Days 1-5 (3 grace days through day 8)
- ❑ 14 Day PPS Assessment – ARD Days 11-14 (5 grace days through day 19, only if assessment is not combined with initial OBRA assessment. If combined, ARD must be before day 14.)
- ❑ 30 Day PPS Assessment – ARD Days 21-29 (5 grace days through day 34)
- ❑ 60 Day PPS Assessment – ARD Days 50-59 (5 grace days through day 64)
- ❑ 90 Day PPS Assessment – ARD Days 80-89 (5 grace days through day 94, only if assessment is not combined with quarterly OBRA assessment. If combined, ARD must be by day 92)

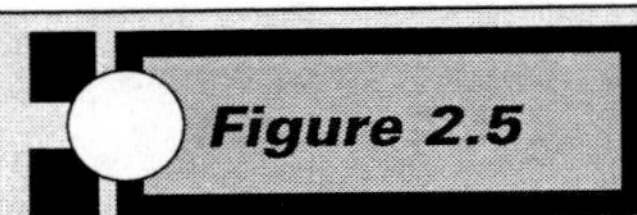

Medicare Part A technical review

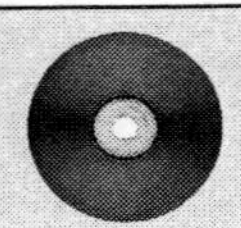

RESIDENT:

GOAL: Review of UB-92 and medical record to ensure that the UB-92 is correct and is supported by the medical record documentation.

TECHNICAL ELIGIBILITY				
ITEM	DOCUMENT	MET	NOT MET	COMMENTS
1. Admission/Readmission Date	MDS, Orders			
2. Medicare enrollment verified	CWF or MC card			
3. Resident's information correct on UB-92 and matches source document				
➢ Name (FL# 12)	CWF or MC card			
➢ Date of birth (FL# 14)	CWF or MC card			
➢ Sex (FL# 15)	CWF or MC card			
➢ Admission date (FL# 17)	Admit face sheet			
➢ HIC number (FL# 60)	CWF or MC card			
3. Medicare Secondary Payer (MSP) Questionnaire completed	MSP Questionnaire or CWF			
4. Three-day qualifying hospital stay	Admit face sheet			
5. Thirty-day transfer requirement	CWF or admit face sheet			
6. Physician certification/recertification completed per regulations				
➢ Completed timely	Cert/recert form			
➢ Signed by physician	Cert/recert form			
➢ Contained required content	Cert/recert form			
7. Ancillary orders signed prior to claim submission				
➢ Physical Therapy	Orders			
➢ Occupational Therapy	Orders			
➢ Speech Therapy	Orders			
➢ Enterals	Orders			
➢ Medical Supplies	Orders			
➢ X-ray	Orders			
➢ Labs	Orders			
➢ Orthotics/Prosthetics	Orders			
8. All ancillary charges reflected on UB-92	Orders			
9. Bill type FL#4 and Status Code FL#22 are correct	UB-92 instructions			

MDS/UB-92 CONSISTENCY				
ITEM	DOCUMENTATION	MET	NOT MET	COMMENTS
1. Number of covered days in FL#7 matches total units in FL#46	UB-92			
2. RUG-III per MDS and assessment type = UB-92 FL #44 (i.e., RMC01)				
➢ Initial/five-day assessment	MDS Sections T3 and A3a & b			
➢ 14-day assessment	MDS Sections T3 and A3a & b			
➢ 30-day assessment	MDS Sections T3 and A3a & b			
➢ 60-day assessment	MDS Sections T3 and A3a & b			
➢ 90-day assessment	MDS Sections T3 and A3a & b			
3. Assessment reference date per MDS = UB-92 service date FL#45 (i.e., 6/14/02)				
➢ Initial/five-day assessment	MDS Section A3a			
➢ 14-day assessment	MDS Section A3a			
➢ 30-day assessment	MDS Section A3a			
➢ 60-day assessment	MDS Section A3a			
➢ 90-day assessment	MDS Section A3a			
4. Rehab RUG III per MDS = UB-92 FL#44				
5-day assessment	MDS Section A3a			

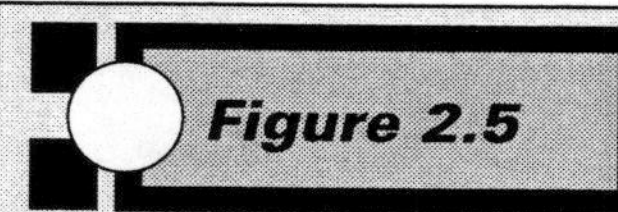

Figure 2.5

Medicare Part A technical review (cont.)

➢ 14-day assessment	MDS Section A3a			
➢ 30-day assessment	MDS Section A3a			
➢ 60-day assessment	MDS Section A3a			
➢ 90-day assessment	MDS Section A3a			
5. Therapy minutes per treatment progress notes (grid) = MDS section P1b				
➢ Physical Therapy	Progress notes (grid)			
➢ Occupational Therapy	Progress notes (grid)			
➢ Speech Therapy	Progress notes (grid)			
➢ Section T				
6. Therapy minutes per treatment progress notes (grid) = therapy billing treatment log (1 unit 8 to < 23 min; 2 units 23 < 38 min; 3 units 38 to < 53 min; 4 units 53 to < 68 min.)				
➢ Physical Therapy	Progress notes (grid and treatment log)			
➢ Occupational Therapy	Progress notes (grid and treatment log)			
➢ Speech Therapy	Progress notes (grid and treatment log)			
7. Therapy units per therapy billing treatment log = UB-92 FL#46 (1 unit 8 to < 23 min; 2 units 23 < 38 min; 3 units 38 to < 53 min; 4 units 53 to < 68 min.)				
➢ Physical Therapy	Treatment log			
➢ Occupational Therapy	Treatment log			
➢ Speech Therapy	Treatment log			
8. Validation report received for each MDS	Validation report			
9. Resident physician on UB-92 FL#82 is correct	Medical record			
10. Principle diagnosis on UB-92 Fl#67 = admission order sheet and MDS Section I (MDS does not need to be sequenced)	Medical record and MDS Section I			
11. Diagnosis sequencing for first five codes on UB-92 FL#67-71 = admission order sheet and MDS Section I (MDS does not need to be sequenced)	Medical record and MDS Section I			

MEDICAL NECESSITY AND SUPPORTING DOCUMENTATION				
ITEM	DOCUMENTATION	MET	NOT MET	COMMENTS
12. Medical Necessity				
➢ Physician Notes				
➢ Physician Orders				
➢ Nursing Notes				
➢ Therapy Notes				
➢ Other Notes				
13. ADL Documentation				
➢ Bed Mobility				
➢ Transfers				
➢ Eating				
➢ Toileting				

REIMBURSEMENT				
ITEM	DOCUMENTATION	MET	NOT MET	COMMENTS
14. Expected Reimbursement				
15. R/A Date				
16. Amount Received				
17. Co-Insurance				
18. Total				
19. Overpayment				
20. Overpayment				

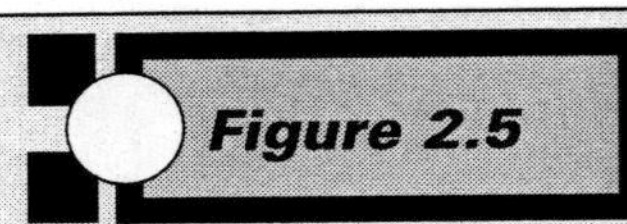

Medicare Part A technical review (cont.)

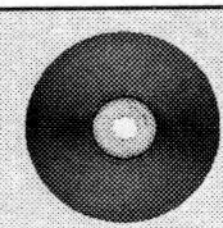

X - Met or not met
NA - Not applicable
NR - Not reviewed

ADDITIONAL CORRECTIONS NEEDED, RESPONSIBLE PERSONS, DUE DATE (SEE COMMENTS SECTION ABOVE):

REVIEWER:	TITLE:	REVIEW DATE:
REVIEWER:	TITLE:	REVIEW DATE:
REVIEWER:	TITLE:	REVIEW DATE:

FILE AUDIT WITH CORRECTIONS AND SUBMIT TO QI COMMITTEE.

Source: Sheila Banducci, RN, MSN, CRRN, president of Savvy Senior Solutions, Inc. Used with permission.

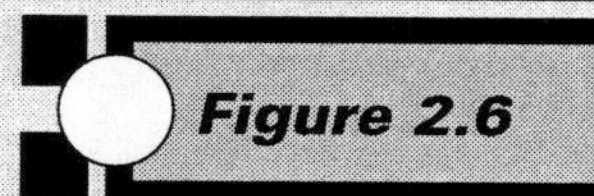

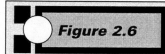

Figure 2.6 Medicare certification and MDS audit

By:			Date:
Resident:	YES	NO	COMMENT:
Physician certification/recertification:			
1. Completed in a timely manner:			
2. Signed by authorized physician:			
3. Contains required content:			
MDS Timing/Scheduling			
1. ARD set within required parameters:			
2. AA9 signatures (interdisciplinary team completion of sections) are after the ARD: 3. R2b/Vb2 dates (assessment coordinator) on or after last AA9 date:			
4. R2b/Vb2 dates are no more than 14 days after ARD:			
5. Vb4 date (care plan completion) is no more than 7 days after VB2:			
6. Initial admission assessment completed (Vb2) is no later than day 14:			
7. OMRA: ARD 8 to 10 days after all therapy is discharged and resident remains skilled by nursing:			
8. Transmitted no more than 31 days after R2b (Medicare) or Vb4 (OBRA):			
9. Use of the grace days is appropriate:			
10. Printed copy of current MDS is located in the resident's chart:			
11. 15 months of MDSs are located in the chart or available at the Nurse's station:			
12. Section P1b therapy days and minutes match the therapy progress notes:			

NOTE: Complete RAP SUMMARY AND CARE PLAN AUDIT

Source: Sheila Banducci, RN, MSN, CRRN, president of Savvy Senior Solutions, Inc. Used with permission.

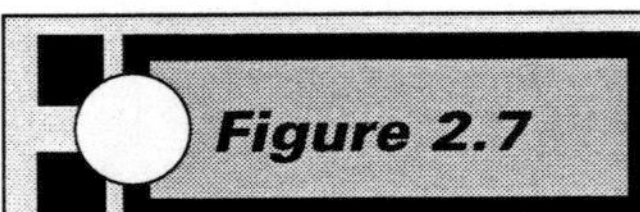

Compliance form

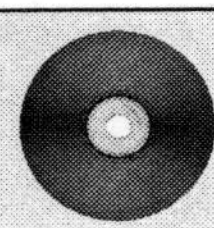

Univ # ________ Claim #: ________ Patient Identification: ________________ Audit Date: ________________

Medicare Number: ________________ Facility: ________________ Provider #:

							(ADL Scores)			
5-Day	**MDS**	Admit Date	ARD	# of grace days	RUG	Reason for Assess/HIPPS	Bed Mobility A	Transfers B	Eating H	Toileting I
ARD & Use of Grace days										
ICD-9 Codes on MDS										
Supported in Chart										

(Expected Look Back Period)

Therapy Minutes	From	Thru	MDS Days	MDS Minutes	Actual Days	Actual Min	Orders Y/N	Section T Complete/Correct
Speech								
Occupational Therapy								
Physical Therapy								
Respiratory Therapy								
Section P Special Treatme								

							(ADL Scores)			
14-Day	**MDS**	Admit Date	ARD	# of grace days	RUG	Reason for Assess/HIPPS	Bed Mobility A	Transfers B	Eating H	Toileting I
ARD & Use of Grace days										
ICD-9 Codes on MDS										
Supported in Chart										

(Expected Look Back Period)

Therapy Minutes	From	Thru	MDS Days	MDS Minutes	Actual Days	Actual Min	Orders Y/N		
Speech									
Occupational Therapy									
Physical Therapy									
Respiratory Therapy									
Section P Special Treatme									

							(ADL Scores)			
30-Day	**MDS**	Admit Date	ARD	# of grace days	RUG	Reason for Assess/HIPPS	Bed Mobility A	Transfers B	Eating H	Toileting I
ARD & Use of Grace days										
ICD-9 Codes on MDS										
Supported in Chart										

(Expected Look Back Period)

Therapy Minutes	From	Thru	MDS Days	MDS Minutes	Actual Days	Actual Min	Orders Y/N		
Speech									
Occupational Therapy									
Physical Therapy									
Respiratory Therapy									
Section P Special Treatme									

Additional Information:

Univ. # ________ Claim #: ________ Patient Identification: ________________ Audit Date: ________________

Medicare Number: ________________ Facility: ________________ Provider #: ________________

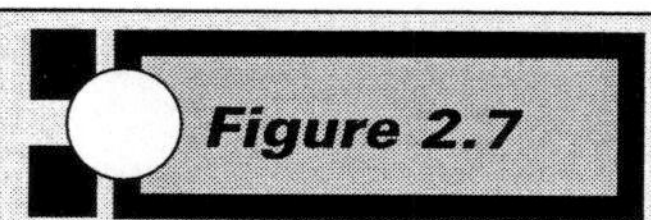

Figure 2.7 Compliance form (cont.)

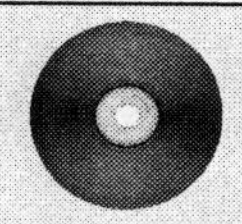

Admission Information

Physician Certification Dates Admission ________ 14 Day ________ 44 Day ________ 74 Day ________

MSP Form	YES	NO	N/A
Medicare Denial Notice	YES	NO	N/A
Other________________	YES	NO	N/A

UB92 INFORMATION

Admit Date	From Date	Thru Date	Bill Type	DC Status
RUG/HIPPS	ARD	DAYS BILLED	Daily Rate	Expect Reimb
				$0.00
				$0.00
				$0.00
				$0.00
				$0.00
			Total Expected:	$0.00

(Qualify StayDates)

From Date	Thru Date		
R/A Date	Amt Rcvd	Co-ins Amt	Total
		$0.00	$0.00

Paid Correctly YES ____ NO ____

Correct $ Amount	$ Overpaid	$ Underpaid

	TX Units of Serv	Calc Minutes (UnitsX15)	Documented TX Minutes	Eval Billed	Eval Documented	Notes
Physical Therapy						
Occupational Therap						
Speech						
Respiratory Therapy						

Consolidated Billing						
Supported in Records						

ICD-9 Codes on UB									
Supported in Chart									

Additional Notes:

____

____

____

____

Reviewers Name (Please Print) ______________________ **Signature:** ______________________

Source: Becky Carroll, RN, MS, vice president of HFS Consultants in Oakland, CA. Used with permission.

Auditing for preadmission screening

Preadmission screening for residents proposed to be covered under Medicare Part A helps ensure appropriate reimbursement. Under some circumstances, coverage may be based on care and services captured in the lookback into the hospital under the administrative presumption of coverage. Under this regulation, when a resident correctly classifies into one of the upper 35 RUG categories on the Medicare 5-day assessment, the level of care criteria are assumed to be met through the ARD of the 5-day assessment. Thus, coverage until that time may be based solely on services captured in the lookback to the hospital. Ensure that appropriate documentation of those services appears in the resident's chart in the SNF.

Also, it is important for the SNF staff to understand the medical necessity for skilled rehabilitation on admission. Based on a resident's prior level of function, physical condition, and reasons for functional decline, skilled rehab may or may not be justifiable. Thus, it is important to conduct audits of the preadmission process relative to skilled services. See Figure 2.8 for a preadmission screening tool.

Auditing for consolidated billing

Consolidated billing is the 1998 provision of the Social Security Act that requires SNFs to include on their bills to Medicare almost all of the services that a resident receives during a Part A stay—whether the services are provided in the facility or off-site.

In the past, vendors who provided supplies, equipment, or services to Part A residents could bill Medicare Part B directly for reimbursement, and facilities had no role in this process. A primary reason for the change is that payment for everything covered under the extended care benefit—with a few notable exceptions—is factored into the facility's daily reimbursement under the SNF PPS. The net effect is that, with a few exceptions, the facility must itself pay any vendor that provides supplies, equipment, or services because the facility is considered to have been paid by Medicare for the services via the PPS per diem.

The complicating factor for SNF providers as well as for outside suppliers of radiology, laboratory, ambulance, DME, and outpatient services is in figuring out what services are excluded from consolidated billing and therefore are billable by the outside entity to Medicare Part B. The law identifies specific categories of services that may be excluded and, in some cases, they are excluded only when provided by a Medicare participating hospital. (See Table 2.1).

Also, within each category, only certain specific services, supplies, or equipment are actually excluded. To determine whether the specific item or service required by the resident is excluded and therefore billable to Part B by the provider of the item or service, SNF providers must research the specific Healthcare Common Procedure Coding System (HCPCS) code to find out who is responsible for billing Medicare. This information, including annual updates to the exclusions list, can be found on the CMS Web site at *www.cms.hhs.gov/snfconsolidatedbilling/80_2006_FI_update.asp.*

Consolidated billing applies to services that are not on the excluded list even when they are provided in association with a visit to a physician's office (although the physician's services are excluded) or a clinic. In addition, as long as the resident remains on Medicare Part A, consolidated billing applies to any services not on the excluded list when the resident is on a leave of absence and arranges for the services himself or herself.

Because of this responsibility of the SNF to pay for services that are not excluded from consolidated billing, nursing homes must have a formal or informal arrangement with providers of these types of services. SNF providers also must inform the resident and outside caregivers, as well as physicians and other healthcare providers, that they must notify the SNF before any such services are provided.

To help SNFs with these notification responsibilities, CMS has provided some best practice guidelines, including sample agreements and communication tools. Also included is a flow chart to assist SNF providers with processing claims from vendors, starting with determining whether the SNF is responsible for payment. They can be found at *www.cms.hhs.gov/SNFPPS/08_BestPractices.asp.* See Figure 2.9 for a chart of how to determine which entity is responsible for a Medicare resident's bill. See Figure 2.10 for a retrospective audit for consolidated billing.

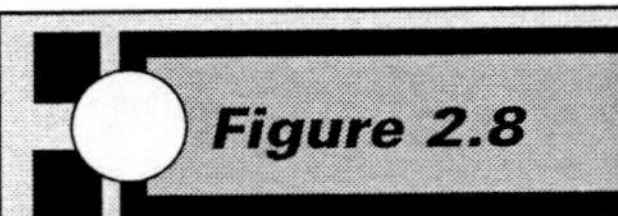

Figure 2.8 Preadmission screening audit for skilled services

Resident's Name______________________ Date of Admission______________
Diagnosis______________________ Auditor______________
Date of Audit______________________ RUG Level______________

Instructions: Checkmark all services provided in hospital and audit SNF record for compliance

Skilled Nursing Service	✓	Last day service received	Location/type of documentation verifying service received in hospital	Signature or name of hospital professional staff providing info appears in SNF chart (yes/no)	Comments
Parenteral/IV					
IV Medication					
Suctioning					
Tracheostomy care					
Ventilator or respirator					
Chemotherapy					
Dialysis					
Oxygen therapy					
Radiation					
Transfusions					
Enteral feeding/TPN					
Wound care					
IM injections					
Suprapubic cath					
Infection/fever					
Other:					
Other:					

Skilled Rehabilitation – Services to be provided in SNF only		
Reason for rehab		
Description of medical necessity		
Reason condition will not spontaneously resolve without the skills of a therapist		

Source: Rena R. Shephard, RRS Healthcare Consulting Services. Used with permission.

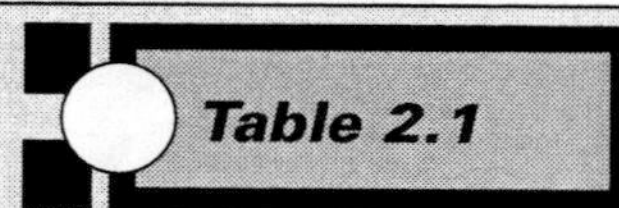

Table 2.1 Major category explanation for SNF consolidated billing

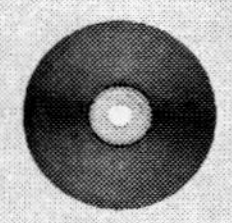

General Explanation of the Major Categories for Skilled Nursing Facility (SNF) Consolidated Billing

Source: CMS website at
http://www.cms.hhs.gov/SNFConsolidatedBilling/Downloads/06MajorCategoryExplanation.pdf

The SNF annual update file contains a comprehensive list of HCPCS codes involved in editing claims submitted to FIs for services subject to SNF consolidated billing (CB). The CMS has divided these codes into 5 Major Categories.

General explanation of the Categories:

Major Category I - **Exclusion of Services Beyond the Scope of a SNF**

These services must be provided on an outpatient basis at a hospital, including a critical access hospital (CAH) only, **not by a SNF,** and are excluded from SNF PPS and CB for beneficiaries in a Part A stay. Services directly related to these services, defined as services billed for the same place of service and with the same line item date of service as the services listed below, are also excluded from SNF CB, with exceptions as listed below.

- Note that anesthesia, drugs incident to radiology and supplies (**revenue codes 037x, 025x, 027x and 062x**) will be bypassed by enforcement edits when billed with CT Scans, Cardiac Catheterizations, MRIs, Radiation Therapies, or Angiographies or surgeries.

- In general, bypasses also allow CT Scans, Cardiac Catheterization, MRI, Radiation Therapy, Angiography, and Outpatient Surgery **HCPCS codes 0001T – 0021T, 0024T – 0026T, or 10021 - 69990** (except HCPCS codes listed as inclusions under Major Category I.F) to process and pay. This includes all other revenue code lines on the incoming claim that have the same line item date of service (LIDOS).

Major Category I is further broken down into subcategories:

A. Computerized Axial Tomography (CT) Scans
B. Cardiac Catheterization
C. Magnetic Resonance Imaging (MRIs)
D. Radiation Therapy
E. Angiography, Lymphatic, Venous and Related Procedures
F. Outpatient Surgery and Related Procedures– INCLUSION (see note below)

Note: Inclusions, rather than exclusions, are given in this one case, because of the great number of surgery procedures that are excluded and can only be safely performed in a hospital operating room setting. It is easier to automate edits around the much shorter list of inclusions under this category, representing **minor procedures that can be performed in the SNF itself.** Additionally, this was the approach originally taken in regulation to present this information. *Procedures associated with splints and casts* are included with minor surgical procedures and appear *with an asterisk (*).*

G. Emergency Services

These services are identified on claims submitted to FIs by a hospital or CAH using **revenue code 045x** (Emergency Room—"x" represents a varying third digit). Related services with the same line item date of service (LIDOS) are also excluded. Note that in order to get a match on the LIDOS there must **be** a LIDOS and HCPCS in revenue code 045x.

H. Ambulance Trips – With Application to Major Category II

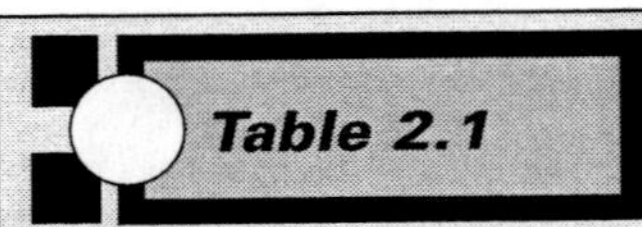

Major category explanation for SNF consolidated billing (cont.)

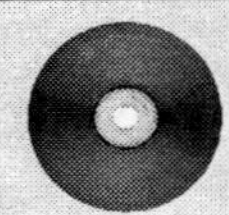

Note: Ambulance trips associated with Major Category I.A-E and G services are excluded from SNF CB. In addition, ambulance trips associated with Major Category II. A. services provided in renal dialysis facilities (RDFs) are also excluded from SNF consolidated billing.

Major Category II - Additional Services Excluded when Rendered to Specific Beneficiaries

These services must be provided to specific beneficiaries, either: (A) End Stage Renal Disease (ESRD) beneficiaries, or (B) beneficiaries who have elected hospice, by specific licensed Medicare providers, and are excluded from SNF PPS and consolidated billing. **SNFs will not be paid for Category II.A. services** (dialysis, etc.) when the SNF is the place of service, as to receive Medicare payment, these services must be provided in a renal dialysis facility. Hospices must also be the only type of provider billing hospice services.

A. Dialysis, EPO, Aranesp, and Other Dialysis Related Services for ESRD Beneficiaries

Specific coding is used to differentiate dialysis and related services that are excluded from SNF consolidated billing for ESRD beneficiaries in three cases: (1) when the services are provided in a RDF (including ambulance services listed under Major Category I. above), (2) home dialysis when the SNF constitutes the home of the beneficiary, and (3) when the drugs EPO or Aranesp are used for ESRD beneficiaries. *Note that SNFs may not be paid for home dialysis supplies.*

Note: Providers/Suppliers may bill their intermediary or carrier for an ESRD-related diagnostic test , provided the test is outside of the ESRD-facility composite rate. The use of the "CB" modifier would allow these services to be bypassed from the SNF CB edits. Please refer to Change Request 2475 for greater detail.

1. Coding Applicable to Services Provided in a RDF

Institutional dialysis services billed only by a RDF are identified by **type of bill 72X.** Services for Method 2 ESRD beneficiaries billed by a RDF must be accompanied by the dialysis related **diagnosis code 585.6.**

1. and 2. Coding Applicable to Services Provided in a RDF or SNF as Home

RDFs, or suppliers only when billing for home dialysis services for beneficiaries who reside in the SNF, use the following **revenue codes** for such billing:

- **825** – Hemodialysis OPD/Home Support Services
- **835** – Peritoneal OPD/Home Support Services
- **845** – Continuous Ambulatory Peritoneal Dialysis OPD/HomeSupport Services
- **855** – Continuous Cycling Peritoneal Dialysis OPD/HomeSupport Services

NOTE: HCPCS codes recognized for use with these revenue codes are identified in the excel file as **Dialysis Supplies** and **Dialysis Equipment.**

3. Coding Applicable to EPO and Aranesp Services

Epoetin alfa (trade name EPO) is a drug Medicare approved for use by ESRD beneficiaries. Intermediary Epoetin alfa claims for ESRD beneficiaries are identified with the following **revenue codes when services are provided in an RDF or Hospital (effective 4/1/06):**

- **634** - EPO with less than 10,000 units)
- **635** - EPO with 10,000 or greater units)

Darbepoetin alfa (trade name Aranesp) is a drug Medicare approved for use by ESRD beneficiaries. Darbepoetin alfa will always be billed in revenue code 636. The HCPCS codes for darbepoetin alfa for ESRD beneficiaries are:

- **Q4054** – for claims with dates of service prior to 1/1/06 or;

Table 2.1 Major category explanation for SNF consolidated billing (cont.)

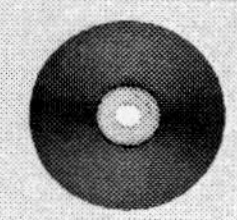

- ☐ **J0882** - for claims with dates of service on or after 1/1/06.

NOTE: When epoetin alfa or darbepoetin alfa are given by the dialysis facility in conjunction with dialysis, these drugs are excluded.

In addition, the HCPCS codes for EPO for ESRD beneficiaries are: **Q4055** – for claims with dates of service prior to 1/1/06 or; **J0886** – for claims with dates of service on or after 1/1/06.

NOTE: See IOM 100-04, Chapter 8, Section 60.4.3.1 for proper billing of EPO in other settings. http://www.cms.hhs.gov/manuals/104_claims/clm104c08.pdf

To distinguish epoetin alfa or darbepoetin alfa given to ESRD beneficiaries from the same drugs given to non-ESRD beneficiaries CMS has developed separate codes.

- ☐ Epoetin for **non-ESRD** beneficiaries is shown with HCPCS code **Q0136** (prior to 1/1/06) and **J0885** (effective 1/1/06), and;
- ☐ Darbepoetin alfa for **non-ESRD** beneficiaries is shown with HCPCS code **Q0137** (prior to 1/1/06) and **J0881** (effective 1/1/06).

NOTE: These codes, like those for ESRD beneficiaries are billed in **revenue code 0636.** These non-ESRD codes are always bundled to the SNF for beneficiaries in a covered Part A stay.

B. Hospice Care for a Beneficiary's Terminal Illness

Hospice services for terminal conditions are identified with the following **bill types: 81X or 82X.**

Major Category III - Additional Excluded Services Rendered by Certified Providers

These services may be provided by any Medicare provider licensed to provide them, **except a SNF,** and are excluded from SNF PPS and consolidated billing.

HCPCS code ranges for chemotherapy, chemotherapy administration, radioisotopes and customized prosthetic devices are set in statute. This statute also gives the Secretary authority to make modifications in the particular codes that are designated for exclusion within each of these service categories; accordingly, the minor and conforming changes in coding that appear in the instruction are made under that authority.

A. Chemotherapy

B. Chemotherapy Administration

Note: Chemotherapy Administration codes listed with an asterisk (*) in the file are included in SNF PPS payment for beneficiaries in a Part A stay when performed alone or with other surgery, but are excluded if they occur with the same line item date of service as an excluded chemotherapy agent. A chemotherapy agent must also be billed when billing these services and physician orders must exist to support the provision of chemotherapy. Codes listed without an asterisk (*) are excluded surgery codes for hospitals, including CAHs, and may be billed without a chemotherapy agent.

C. Radioisotopes and their Administration

D. Customized Prosthetic Devices

Major Category IV - Additional Excluded Preventive and Screening Services

These services are covered as Part B benefits and are not included in SNF PPS. **Such services must be billed by the SNF for beneficiaries in a Part A stay with Part B eli gibility on type of bill (TOB) 22x.** Swing Bed providers must use TOB 12x for eligible beneficiaries in a Part A SNF level.

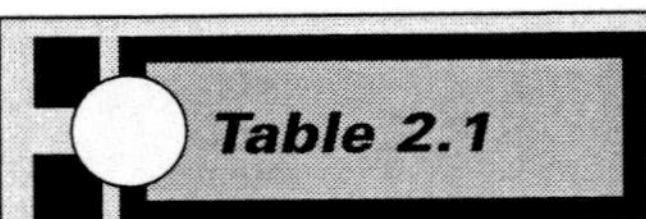

Major category explanation for SNF consolidated billing (cont.)

Note: Please access Chapter 18 "Preventive and Screening Services" of the Claims Processing manual for coverage and billing guidance.

- **A. Mammography**
- **B. Vaccines (Pneumococcal, Flu or Hepatitis B)**
- **C. Vaccine Administration**
- **D. Screening Pap Smear and Pelvic Exams**
- **E. Colorectal Screening Services**
- **F. Prostate Cancer Screening**
- **G. Glaucoma Screening**
- **H. Diabetic Screening**
- **I. Cardiovascular Screening**
- **J. Initial Preventative Physical Exam**

Major Category V - **Part B Services Included in SNF Consolidated Billing**

Therapy services are included in SNF PPS and consolidated billing for residents in a Part A stay, and **must be billed by the SNF alone for its Part B residents and non-residents.**

- **A. Therapies billed with revenues codes 42x (physical therapy), 43x (occupational therapy), 44x (speech-language pathology)**

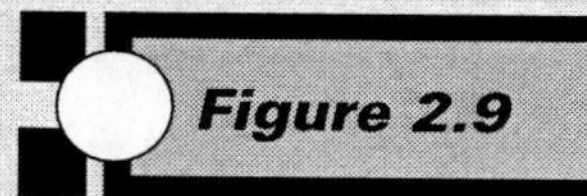

Figure 2.9 SNF responsibilities for consolidated billing

1. Notify outside provider prior to rendering services that it will be treating a resident in a Part A stay.
2. Notify all community vendors of plan and method of communication prior to services being rendered.
3. Designate a staff person to be the gatekeeper for Part A/B residents who are leaving the building to ensure compliance and communication prior to services being rendered. The administrator is responsible for maintaining contracts/agreements with all local outside/inside providers/vendors.
4. Determine whether the vendor understands what its responsibilities are related to the regulations as a Medicare provider. Offer materials available.
5. Determine whether the vendor understands that it will need to notify the SNF prior to rendering services—if it does not, you may not be under obligation to pay. For example, performing a CT scan at the office when CMS requires it to be done at an outpatient hospital for it to be excluded from consolidated billing may not be reimbursable.
6. Pay the physician/vendor for included services in a timely manner.
7. Ensure that the contract includes information related to paying the Medicare fee schedule and/or percentage of fee schedule.
8. Verify that all healthcare vendors are billing the SNF using the itemized HCPC codes.
9. Determine which services are the responsibility of the SNF using the annual consolidated billing update for fiscal intermediaries at *www.cms.hhs.gov/SNFConsolidatedBilling/01_Overview.asp.*
10. Determine medical necessity of services and whether services ordered meet CMS criteria. For example, verify necessity of lab/x-rays ordered when they were just done at the hospital, and inform the physician.

Source: Darla K. Watson, RN, RAC-C, president of Starpointe Healthcare Consulting. Used with permission.

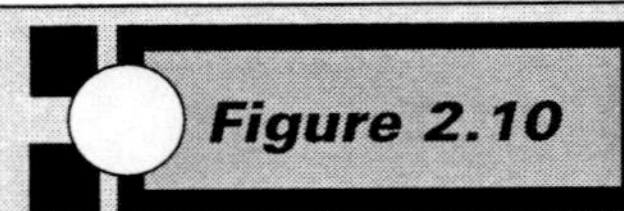

Retrospective audit for consolidated billing

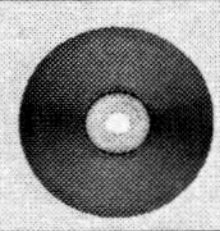

Resident's Name________________________________ Date of Services______________
Outside provider's name____
Services Rendered____
____
____
____

Questions pertain to services provided by outside provider, vendor, supplier, etc.	Yes	No	Comments
1. Physician office, outpatient hospital, clinic, etc., was notified by the SNF in advance that resident is in Part A stay.			
2. HCPCS codes for services to be delivered were requested from physician office, outpatient hospital, clinic, etc., prior to services being rendered.			
3. SNF determined if services were included or excluded prior to services being rendered by outside provider.			
4. SNF verified medical necessity of planned services by outside provider that were not excluded prior to services being rendered.			
5. Physician office, outpatient hospital, clinic, etc., was notified to inform SNF prior to rendering services not already researched by SNF.			
6. Resident and significant others notified prior to visit to outside vendor or LOA to inform SNF if resident requires health care services when out of the facility, other than those already discussed with them.			
7. Services excluded only when rendered by hospital outpatient department were rendered in that setting.			
8. The arrangement with the supplier specifies: a. The arranged-for services for which the SNF assumes responsibility, and b. The manner in which the SNF will pay the supplier for those services.			
9. No services included in consolidated billing were rendered by an outside provider without knowledge and consent of SNF provider			

Conclusion:
Services included in consolidated billing _____ were _____ were not provided by an outside provider/vendor/supplier without knowledge and consent of the SNF provider.

Notes:
____
____
____
____

Source: Rena R. Shephard, RRS Healthcare Consulting Services. Used with permission.

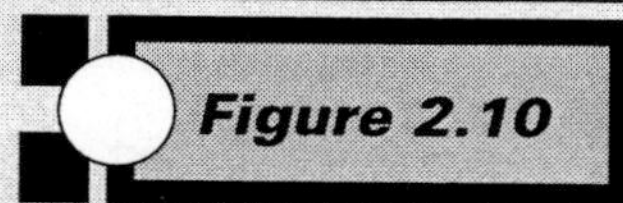

Figure 2.10 Retrospective audit for consolidated billing (cont.)

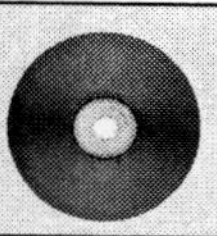

Facility____________________

Resident Name ________________ Admission date__________

Claim service date/RUG ________/________Discharge date________

MDS ARD/RUG _______/_______ Claim from and to dates________

Prior Level of Function: ____________________

Rehab potential: ____________________

Diagnoses:

Skilled Service(s) | Physician's Orders

MDS and Supporting Documentation

Skilled Service(s) | Physician's Orders

MDS and Supporting Documentation

Findings:

Approved
RUG category days x rate = $$

Denied
RUG category days x rate = $$

Reviewer______________Date______

Source: Rena R. Shephard, RRS Healthcare Consulting Services. Used with permission.

Types of audits

Routine monitoring of MDS accuracy is essential for every facility that is required to complete the MDS. Without such monitoring, the first sign that the systems are not working might come from a surveyor or a fiscal intermediary. With routine, ongoing monitoring, however, problems can be identified early, which gives the provider the opportunity to intervene and improve the systems before major problems arise.

The types of audits to complete and the frequency of those audits depend on the needs of the facility. The amount of information on the MDS is extensive, and trying to monitor the accuracy of every item on a routine basis is likely to be overwhelming and difficult or impossible to manage. Thus, in order for the auditing activities to be meaningful and useful, the first step in the auditing process is to identify the facility's specific auditing needs. This step should begin with a thorough baseline audit of MDS accuracy and related assessment timing and scheduling performance. Once that project is completed, consider the following when making decisions about frequency and type of audits:

- Analysis of the baseline audit
- RAI process deficiencies in recent surveys or complaint investigations
- Recent level of claims review by the fiscal intermediary
- Medicare Part A denial history
- Competency and longevity of MDS staff
- Level of collaboration and cooperation among interdisciplinary team members

Some of the options for auditing follow.

Concurrent reviews

These audits of current residents are performed concurrent to the residents' stays in the nursing facility.

Monthly internal monitoring

For this type of monitoring, individuals who have expertise in the MDS coding rules and who are internal to the organization conduct reviews of current charts. Because of the need for objectivity, the individuals responsible for coding the MDSs in the facility must not be the ones who conduct these audits. The purpose of the audits is to verify accuracy of MDS coding decisions and to validate that the overall clinical record supports the coding decisions.

Decide which MDS items to monitor based on which items are high risk for the facility. Be sure to monitor the items identified as the most error-prone for the industry in general, such as Section G1 and P1b (as discussed in Chapter one). Also monitor whether the assessment reference dates are set appropriately and whether assessments are signed off as complete in a timely manner.

The audit should include items identified as problematic through other sources as well, such as previous facility audits, survey deficiencies, and items that have been noted to cause errors in QI/QMs or QMs due to coding mistakes. In general, a good representative sample of items is the 108 items used in the RUG calculations.

Focused weekly audits

Smaller-scale weekly audits can be critical to preserving the integrity of MDS data. These audits should come into play when routine, general monitoring identifies coding problems or when the facility recognizes that certain items must be audited more often than monthly because of their complexity, previous problems, or other concerns. The focus of these audits is likely to shift over time, depending on current circumstances, but for some key items, the weekly audits should continue indefinitely.

Staff members with little or no involvement with the MDS process can play a central role in these audits. With training and support from an expert consultant and MDS staff, any staff member can become the facility expert on one key MDS item. For example, a charge nurse or a medication and treatment nurse can be trained specifically to audit one item, such as item G1, ADL self-performance and ADL support provided. Then this staff member would audit a small, predetermined number of charts each week to determine the accuracy of the coding. The total number of charts audited in a month would be a representative sample across the facility.

Examples of focused audits can be found in Figures 2.11, 2.12, 2.13, and 2.14.

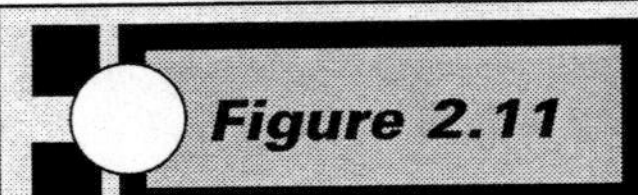

Focused audit for ADLs

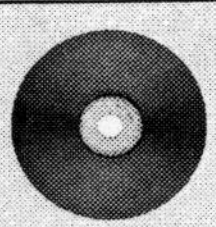

Resident's name________________________________ Date of assessment____________

ADL Focused Audit

INSTRUCTIONS: For each section:

1. **Place a check mark next to the MDS response for this resident in the Resident Data column.**
2. **In the next column, identify the location(s) in the chart where the supporting documentation is located and the date(s) of the entries.**
3. **Discrepancies in the supporting documentation may be appropriate under some circumstances. Where discrepancies exist, mark in the next column if they have been reconciled. ****
4. **In the next column, identify the date the item was completed on this form.**
5. **Place your initials in the Initials column.**

****All discrepancies must be brought to the attention of the Director of Nursing and the Interdisciplinary Team****

MDS Item		Reference window	Resident data	Date and location of supporting documentation	Discrepancies reconciled		Date	Initials
					Yes	No		
G (A). Physical Functioning & Structural Problems ADL Self-performance		7 days						
Bed mobility	Independent							
	Supervision							
	Limited assistance							
	Extensive assistance							
	Total dependence							
	Activity did not occur							
Transfer	Independent							
	Supervision							
	Limited assistance							
	Extensive assistance							
	Total dependence							
	Activity did not occur							
Eating	Independent							
	Supervision							
	Limited assistance							
	Extensive assistance							
	Total dependence							
	Activity did not occur							
Toilet use	Independent							
	Supervision							
	Limited assistance							
	Extensive assistance							
	Total dependence							

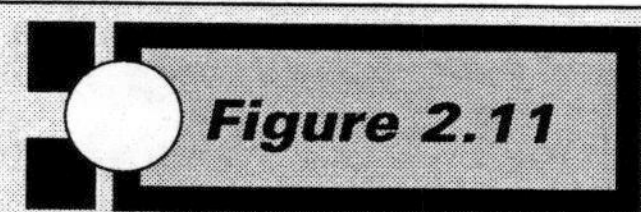

Figure 2.11 Focused audit for ADLs (cont.)

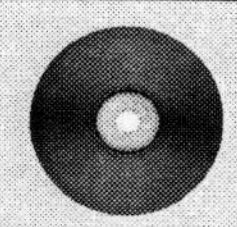

Resident's name____________________ Date of assessment__________

MDS Item		Reference window	Resident data	Date and location of supporting documentation	Discrepancies reconciled		Date	Initials
					Yes	No		
Toilet use (continued)	Activity did not occur							
G(B). Physical Functioning & Structural Problems ADL Support Provided		7 days						
Bed mobility	No setup or physical help							
	Setup help only							
	One person physical assist							
	Two+ person physical assist							
	Activity did not occur at all							
Transfer	No setup or physical help							
	Setup help only							
	One person physical assist							
	Two+ person physical assist							
	Activity did not occur at all							
Eating	No setup or physical help							
	Setup help only							
	One person physical assist							
	Two+ person physical assist							
	Activity did not occur at all							
Toilet use	No setup or physical help							
	Setup help only							
	One person physical assist							
	Two+ person physical assist							
	Activity did not occur at all							

–G9 - Change in ADL function: Is the functional deficit long-standing and/or significant enough to adversely affect rehab potential? No Yes Maybe N/A

Any yes or maybe responses must be brought to the attention of the Director of Nursing and the Interdisciplinary Team.

Signatures of staff completing MDS review:

Initials and Signature ____________ **Title** ____________ **Date** ____________

Initials and Signature ____________ **Title** ____________ **Date** ____________

Initials and Signature ____________ **Title** ____________ **Date** ____________

Source: Rena R. Shephard, RRS Healthcare Consulting Services. Used with permission.

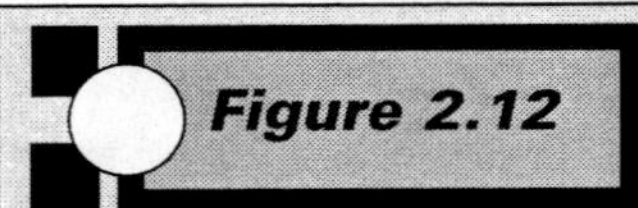

Figure 2.12 MDS timing and scheduling

Requirement	Met	Not met	Comments
1. ARD set within required parameters			
2. AA9 signatures (IDT completion of sections) are on or after ARD			
3. R2b/VB2 dates (assessment coordinator) on or after last AA9 date			
4. R2b/VB2 dates no more than 14 days after ARD for PPS assessments			
5. VB4 date (care plan completion) no more than seven days after VB2			
6. Initial admission assessment completed (V2) no later than day 14			
7. OMRA: ARD day eight to 10 after all therapy discontinued if resident remained skilled			
8. Transmitted no > 31 days after R2b (Medicare) or VB4 (OBRA)			
9. Use of grace days is appropriate			
10. Validation reports verify transmission			

Source: Rena R. Shephard, RRS Healthcare Consulting Services. Used with permission.

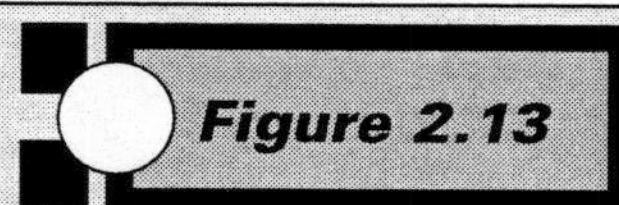

Medicare Part A coverage audit

Skilled Rehabilitation

- Place a checkmark in the center column if documentation related to the criterion supports the need for skilled rehabilitation.
- Place a ø in the center column if documentation related to the criterion does not support the need for skilled rehabilitation.

Coverage Concepts for Consideration	✓ or Ø	Provide brief description of the resident's status in the context of each concept and identify the location the clinical record the information can be found
1. Prior level of function – Extent of functional decline related to this illness/injury warrants skilled rehab		
2. Underlying cause for the decline in function		
3. Underlying physiological reason for the need for skilled rehab		
4. Expectation that condition will not spontaneously resolve with supportive care		
5. Expectation that condition will improve materially in a reasonable amount of time and in a generally predictable amount of time		
6. Services are needed at a level of complexity and sophistication, or the condition of the patient must be of a nature that requires the judgment, knowledge, and skills of a qualified therapist		
7. Treatment must be consistent with the nature and severity of the illness or injury		
8. Concept of "reasonable and necessary": Expected results must be significant in relation to extent and duration of the services required to achieve those results		
9. Significant and reasonably consistent progress?		

Conclusions:

___

___

___

___

___

Source: Rena R. Shephard, RRS Healthcare Consulting Services. Used with permission.

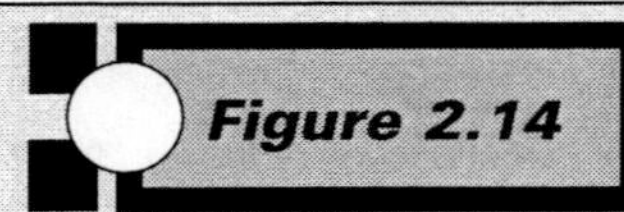

Therapy minutes audit

(See instructions for calculating units below)

Assessment #1

ARD:	MDS	Chart grid	Minutes log	UB-92 units	Discrepancy
PT					
OT					
ST					

Assessment #2

ARD:	MDS	Chart grid	Minutes log	UB-92 units	Discrepancy
PT					
OT					
ST					

Assessment #3

ARD:	MDS	Chart grid	Minutes log	UB-92 units	Discrepancy
PT					
OT					
ST					

Calculating rehab units from minutes

NOTE: Therapy minutes reported on the MDS must be* actual minutes *and not derived from units. Units are calculated from the minutes on the MDS to enter on the UB-92 claim form.

For each rehab discipline, add the **sum of the units per day** for services delivered. Calculate the units as follows:

Bill for 1 unit if the total for the day is > 8 minutes to < 23 minutes
Bill for 2 units if the total for the day is > 23 minutes to < 38 minutes
Bill for 3 units if the total for the day is > 38 minutes to < 53 minutes
Bill for 4 units if the total for the day is > 53 minutes to < 68 minutes
Bill for 5 units if the total for the day is > 68 minutes to < 83 minutes
Bill for 6 units if the total for the day is > 83 minutes to < 98 minutes
Bill for 7 units if the total for the day is > 98 minutes to < 113 minutes
Bill for 8 units if the total for the day is > 113 minutes to < 128 minutes

Source: Rena R. Shephard, RRS Healthcare Consulting Services. Used with permission.

Inter-rater reliability

To test the expertise of your MDS coordinator, two people with expertise in the MDS process independently complete an assessment for the same resident using the same assessment reference date. At least one of the individuals should have primary responsibility for MDS completion in the facility; the other person should have considerable expertise in MDS coding. If the two individuals have a good understanding of the coding rules, and if training has been adequate, the two assessments should yield similar information.

This kind of inter-rater reliability testing is the focus of the DAVE two-staged review described in the Introduction.

Retrospective reviews

Retrospective reviews are audits of closed records, which may include old records for current long-term residents. They provide valuable information about practices and trends related to MDS processes and accuracy.

Routine external auditing

Often, internal auditing is carried out by employees of the facility or, for multiple-facility organizations, by regional or corporate staff. Such auditing is crucial to achieve and maintain MDS coding compliance and accuracy. However, it is equally important for MDS accuracy to be reviewed by the objective eyes of experts who are not part of the organization. In retaining experts to carry out this function, nursing home organizations should thoroughly validate the credentials, experience, and expertise of the individuals involved.

External audits may involve concurrent as well as retrospective reviews in order to assess the accuracy and appropriateness of assessments over time. They also should focus on the timeliness of assessments and examine whether off-cycle assessments, such as the OMRA and the SCSA, are used appropriately.

Routine monitoring of summary online and Web reports

Transmission of MDS data to both the state database and the national repository by more than 17,000 U.S. nursing homes is creating an enormous database of information about residents in nursing homes. As a result, the state system can give providers access to many reports that focus on the numbers and types of assessments submitted, as well as facility and resident characteristics. These reports are in addition to the QI reports discussed in the Introduction, which also provide comparison information relative to the state and the nation.

These reports consist of several scheduled reports made available via the state system each month. You can view samples of these reports at *www.qtso.com/mdsdownload.html.* Although providers might not find a use for each and every one of the 25 reports, many of the reports are ideal for administrators and other members of the administrative team to use in monitoring their MDS completion systems. This chapter discusses how to use the reports.

The following are some of the key reports that can help you audit the integrity of your MDS systems:

- **The End of Month Roster Report:** Lists current residents with the most recent assessment processed by the end of the month. This report can help identify missed assessments.

- **Resident Discharged without Return:** Lists residents discharged with return anticipated but who did not return. If the resident will not be returning, the option is to complete a second tracking form to eliminate the resident from the system.

- **The MDS Activity Report:** Includes all assessments submitted in the previous month. This is the only report that includes RUG levels, and it should be used to validate that

  - the RUG levels calculated by the facility's MDS software match the RUG levels calculated by the state. This report also should be provided to the billing office each month so the RUG levels billed can be checked against it.

  - MDSs are being submitted.

  - Certain assessment types—such as off-cycle assessments, including OMRAs and SCSAs—are being submitted.

- **The New Admission Report:** Includes all new admissions in the previous month. This report should be used to verify that OBRA- and PPS-required assessments are being completed.

- **The Missing Assessment Report:** Lists residents whose most recent assessment (that was not a discharge tracking form) occurred more than 138 days ago. Many of the entries on this list are likely to be residents who were discharged to the hospital with return anticipated but who did not return. However, some of them may represent missed assessments.

A description of all available scheduled reports can be found in Chapter 4 of the *Long Term Care Facility User's Guide*, a manual specific to the automation process, which can be accessed through the MDS transmission screen in the facility or at the bottom of the screen at *www.qtso.com/mdsdownload.html.*

Another set of reports available to providers are the Certification and Survey Provider Enhanced Reports (CASPER). These reports may be requested by providers through the state system at any time. In addition to the QI/QM reports available at this location, some important CASPER reports for providers to monitor are as follows:

- **Reports detailing the warning and fatal file errors received by the facility:** When records are transmitted to the state database, they undergo a series of audits, and the results of the audits (including warnings and fatal file errors) can be found on the Initial Feedback Report and the Final Validation Report.

Although the state system cannot check the accuracy of MDS responses relative to the medical record or to the UB-92 claim form, it can and does conduct consistency, valid value, and range audits. When such errors are detected, a warning message appears on the Final Validation Report. Although an MDS record containing such an error will be accepted into the state database and does not require correction, MDS staff must understand the error and avoid making the error in the future to avoid sending a red flag to the state.

On the other hand, fatal file errors result in the rejection of the entire submission batch. In that case, the individual data records are not validated or stored in the database and they must be corrected and resubmitted.

MDS staff should be familiar with fatal file and warning messages to ensure accuracy. The details of the warning and error messages can be found in the Validation Report Messages and Description Guide, which can be accessed via the facility's transmission screen or at the bottom of the screen at *www.qtso.com/mdsdownload.html*.

- **The Monthly Submission Statistics Report:** It identifies the numbers of records processed, rejected, and accepted. Occasional rejections are expected, but this report should be monitored for signs of problems.
- **The Error Summary Report by Facility:** If the Monthly Submission Statistics report looks suspicious, this report gives more detail about the errors/rejections.
- **Admission/Reentries**.
- **Discharges.**
- **Duplicate Residents.**
- **The Roster Report:** It lists latest information for current residents.
- **Daily Submission Statistics.**
- **Submission Statistics by Facility.**
- **The Vendor List.**
- **RFA Statistics:** This report lists all current assessments by assessment type.

MDS staff and administrative team members should assess the usefulness of all available CASPER reports. More information on these reports can be found at *www.qtso.com/download/mds/ltc/append_b.pdf.*

In addition to the reports available through the state system, commercial MDS software (as opposed to the Raven software provided without charge by CMS) generally can make a plethora of similar reports available. Information about these reports is available from the facility's software vendor.

Unscheduled audits

Each facility should establish a routine schedule of audits based on facility-specific needs and identification of general risk areas. In addition, the facility's policies and procedures should include mechanisms for adding unscheduled audits to the mix based on current information and events.

For example, a complaint investigation by the state agency or a claim review by the fiscal intermediary might identify the need to audit particular MDS items or aspects of the MDS process. Analysis of QI or QM data might point to coding errors that warrant staff training and subsequent monitoring for a period of time. Facility processes should be alert to these kinds of situations and should trigger a system that adds the needed surveillance.

Chapter 3

Conducting audits

Identifying the auditors

Because job descriptions are not standardized across the industry, identifying the individuals or the staff positions responsible for conducting MDS audits is a very facility-specific matter. The single most important factor to consider is the individuals' expertise.

There are two reasons to emphasize expertise. First, audits conducted by individuals who don't have it are unlikely to help the facility in continuous improvement in MDS coding and related activities. Second, the coding, transmission, and billing rules related to the MDS process are quite complex, so it is not sufficient to provide a copy of the *Long Term Care Facility Resident Assessment Instrument User's Manual* and send new auditors on their way. The auditor must be at least as knowledgeable as the experts who complete the form.

Auditors should be chosen by an expert whose competency has already been verified. This expert should evaluate candidates' work and validate their competencies. If that is not possible, however, the facility should provide potential auditors with formal training through a recognized agency or organization, such as the state agency, the state healthcare association, the state's quality improvement organization, or the American Association of Nurse Assessment Coordinators (AANAC).

After completing the program, candidates will need to work alongside MDS staff whose competency has been verified until they grasp the concepts and details of the process. Candidates should not begin auditing activities until they demonstrate to the provider's satisfaction that they have attained the required competency.

It is also important to validate the competency of the individual providing the training and that of the prospective auditor in the case of focused audits, in which a staff member is assigned to develop expertise in one small but critical aspect of MDS coding.

Identifying the charts

The administrative team should determine which charts to audit based on information already known about the MDS processes and MDS accuracy in the facility.

First, management must determine what percentage of charts to audit. For example, a facility with stable and proven MDS and billing staff may only need to audit 5% of charts each month. On the other hand, a facility that already has identified problems with MDS accuracy or that has little information about its MDS accuracy might need to audit 10% per month. Similar decisions must be made about audits focused on one aspect of clinical care and MDS-billing audits.

Once management has decided how many charts to audit, they must choose the charts to audit. They may do so via random sampling—for example, if a facility averages 200 MDS assessments per month and decides on a 10% audit, the 20 assessments can be selected by choosing every tenth assessment on a list of the 200 MDSs. To supplement the random sample, they also might select charts with characteristics identified as high risk to the facility.

Preparing for the audit

Because MDS audits require significant concentration on the part of auditors, provide them with a quiet location in which to conduct it. Make a copy of the most current version of the *Long Term Care Facility Resident Assessment Instrument User's Manual* readily available for them to use.

Auditors should select the audit form that best meets the criteria and goals for the audit they will perform. The form should prompt them to audit specific items and process issues and may provide additional cues about what to look for.

The audit process

Whether they are focused audits involving only one or two MDS sections or are audits of wider scope, MDS accuracy audits should focus on meeting the goals described earlier in this book. The following recommended process for achieving those goals provides for the auditor to review the MDS and related documentation and to research any coding discrepancies.

For each MDS item to be audited, the auditor should follow six steps. The examples used to illustrate audit steps 1–3 focus on items G1b(A) and (B), ADL self-performance and support provided for transfers.

1. Identify the coding decision as entered on the MDS for the particular item. Example: Consult the most recently completed MDS for the resident and identify the coding that was entered for this item. For this example, let's say the coding was "3," extensive assistance for self-performance in column A, and "3," two or more people assisting for support provided in column B.

2. Collect information from throughout the clinical record to determine the correct coding. Include only information from the seven-day observation period that ends with the ARD.

Example: The auditor checks all locations in the record that might refer to the resident's transfer ability. Such locations include licensed nurses notes, nursing assistant notes, restorative nursing notes (if applicable), rehabilitation therapy notes (if applicable), and the care plan. In addition, the assessor should check fall and restraint assessment forms, which might include this type of information, and ancillary department notes for references to transfers during activities or with family members.

3. Based on the information collected, the author should determine whether the clinical record supports the coding on the MDS. Example: The auditor might find that the resident usually transfers with the assistance of one staff member or one family member, who guides him and holds onto the gait belt in case he needs more assistance. However, physical therapy notes indicate that on two occasions the resident lost his balance slightly and required the therapist to provide a minimum level of weight-bearing assistance. Also, a CNA reported early one morning that she unexpectedly had to provide weight-bearing assistance.

Therefore, the conclusion for column A, ADL self-performance, would be that the clinical record supports the coding of extensive assistance.

Regarding column B, ADL support provided for transfers, the record showed from all sources that the resident required the assistance of one person for transfers throughout the observation period, with one exception: On the night shift, the nursing assistant once had to request assistance from another staff member to transfer the resident to the bedside commode and back because the resident was feeling ill.

The conclusion for column B, ADL support provided for transfers, would be that the clinical record supports the MDS coding decision of "3," two or more people assisting.

4. If the clinical record contains conflicting information, determine through further clinical record review whether the discrepancy has been resolved.

Contradictory information among disciplines is common because the performance of residents often varies depending on the time of day, level of fatigue, mood, and other factors. However, when apparently contradictory information appears in the record, the auditor should conduct further review to determine whether the conflict was resolved.

Example: When coding the MDS for walking, if the restorative nursing records reveal that every day the resident is ambulating more 100 ft with oversight assistance only, and the nursing assistants are documenting that the resident requires hands-on physical assistance for walking, this inconsistency does not make sense. It must be resolved before a coding decision can be made.

5. If the clinical record does not support the coding on the MDS, determine the cause through further record review/interview with the staff member who completed the item on the MDS by doing the following:

- Validate that the coding is based on current coding instructions found in the *Long Term Care Facility Resident Assessment Instrument User's Manual.*

- Confirm that MDS coding decisions are based on interviews with the resident (when possible), family members and other significant others, and staff members working with the resident; record review, including all shifts and all disciplines; and direct observation by the assessor.

  Documentation may reveal that the resident's performance varied depending on the shift or the discipline involved. An accurate interpretation of the coding rules should result in a correct coding decision; failure to take into account all relevant information in the clinical record may cause coding errors. Further, the assessor might have failed to document information that went into the coding decision.

- Determine whether the assessor has a clear understanding of the coding rules.

- Verify that the appropriate lookback periods were used for each item. Discrepancies in the coding on the MDS relative to the auditor's determination may reflect use of data that occurred outside of the observation window.

6. Validate that timing and scheduling requirements were met.

Chapter 4

PUTTING AUDIT RESULTS TO WORK

Follow-up of audit results

In nursing homes, various types of clinical record audits are used to verify that care and services are being documented and that problems are being identified for follow-up. The real challenge lies in putting the audit results to work—getting them into the appropriate hands for follow-up on a day-to-day basis and using them to analyze resident care and documentation systems to prevent recurrence of avoidable problems. The same is true of the MDS auditing process.

Because of the large volume of MDS assessments in many facilities, audit results should be reported back to the MDS team as quickly as possible to help limit repetition of problems they identify. If the follow-up process ends there, however, it is unlikely that sustained improvement will result. Therefore, each facility should develop a protocol that identifies the steps to take when deficiencies are noted. The protocol should include provisions for investigation into the root causes of the deficiencies and an action plan targeted at the identified problems.

Clearly, a single approach to resolving every type of deficiency is unlikely to be effective. For example, an action plan designed to eliminate data-entry errors will be very different from a plan to resolve a knowledge deficit on the part of the interdisciplinary team or to redesign an operational system to foster MDS accuracy. Therefore, management needs to consider different approaches to solving data accuracy problems.

After the action plan is implemented, a follow-up audit should be conducted within a defined timeframe to verify that the problems have been resolved. Clear lines of responsibility and accountability should be identified in the protocol.

A suggested protocol for audit follow-up appears in Figure 4.1. A discussion of operational processes that affect MDS accuracy can be found in the Introduction.

Continuous quality improvement

To succeed, individuals and organizations alike must recognize that improvement is always possible, and they should strive to seize any opportunity that will foster improvement. Everyone involved with care and services related to nursing home residents should always be alert to indications that improvements are necessary to the benefit of residents and the organization. From the facility perspective, continuous quality improvement (CQI) should be built into organizational processes in order to ensure that process flaws that can lead to problems are identified early and thus provide the opportunity for intervention before serious problems occur.

The auditing processes and procedures described in this book are ideal sources of information in the context of CQI. They can be integrated into the activities of the facility's quality assessment and assurance committee (QAAC), which can provide valuable oversight and assistance for continuous improvement.

Given the central role of the MDS in the nursing home, providers should consider developing an MDS accuracy committee as a subcommittee of the QAAC. The committee's role would be to track and trend MDS audit deficiencies and action plans over time, to evaluate improvement efforts, and to make recommendations for improvement. Audit results would be reported to the QAAC routinely, and this committee would analyze each type of audit deficiency in the context of previous audit deficiencies in order to identify patterns and causes.

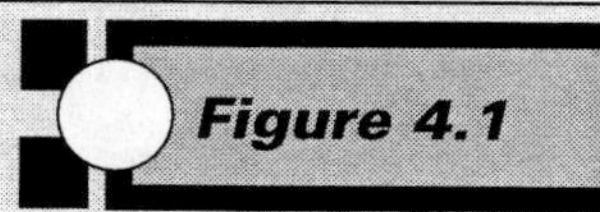

MDS audit deficiency follow-up protocol

1. Upon completion of the audit, the auditor will undertake an analysis of each deficiency in an effort to determine the probable cause(s) of the deficiencies. Possible causes include the following:
   a. Isolated data-entry error
   b. Pattern of data-entry errors
   c. Misinterpretation of chart documentation
   d. Lack of chart documentation
   e. Knowledge deficit on the part of an individual participant in the MDS process regarding MDS coding rules and processes
   f. Knowledge deficit on the part of MDS staff/interdisciplinary team members in general regarding MDS coding rules and processes
   g. Poor interdisciplinary communication/collaboration
   h. Defects in operational systems (to be specified by the auditor)
   i. Other causes (to be specified by the auditor)

2. The auditor will complete a Summary of Findings, including results of the analysis. The Summary of Findings will be attached to the completed audit.

3. A copy of the completed audit will be delivered to the MDS office and will be distributed to the Administrator and the Director of Nursing Services. The auditor will provide copies of the audit to ancillary staff members when deficiencies related to their disciplines are identified.

4. MDS and ancillary staff will review the findings and develop and implement an action plan for immediate corrections (as appropriate) and for avoiding the problem in the future.
   a. This action plan must be submitted to the Administrator, the Director of Nursing, and the auditor within 48 hours of receipt of the audit results.
   b. The action plan will clearly identify the individual(s) responsible for ensuring that improvement takes place.

5. The Administrator and the auditor will review the action plan within 24 hours of receiving it and will
   a. determine the appropriateness of the plan.
   b. add to or revise the plan as necessary.
   c. evaluate the need for operational systems improvement and develop plans for implementing such improvements.

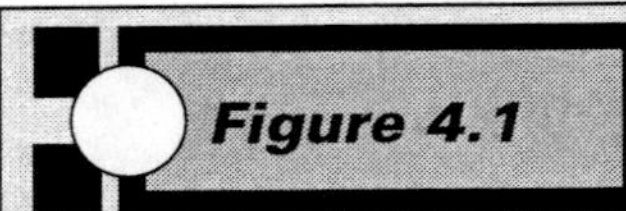

MDS audit deficiency follow-up protocol (cont.)

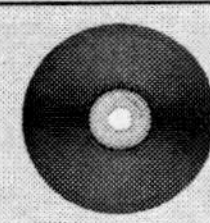

d. determine the need for individual counseling or disciplinary action.

6. The Administrator or his/her designee will provide feedback to the MDS and ancillary staff based on Step 5 above.

7. A focused follow-up audit will be conducted two weeks after the action plan is implemented to verify that the problems have been resolved. If they have not, the process begins again with formal oversight by the Administrator.

8. Audit results and final action plans will be reported to the MDS Accuracy Committee of the Quality Assessment and Assurance Committee. The committee's role is to evaluate improvement efforts, to make recommendations for improvement, and to track and trend deficiencies and action plans over time to assess the overall effectiveness of improvement efforts.

Source: Rena R. Shephard, RRS Healthcare Consulting Services. Used with permission.

In this way, the committee would be able to identify, for example, that Section G1, ADLs, had a significant increase in deficiencies over time, and would be able to correlate that problem with certain personnel changes over time. This subcommittee would be in a good position to evaluate the overall effectiveness of improvement efforts.

Chapter 5

Organizational processes that foster MDS accuracy

Although it is true that individuals can make or break MDS accuracy, it is also true that facility processes either foster or impede efforts toward accuracy and continuous improvement. Because these processes are so influential, developing and managing ones that foster accuracy should be a high priority for everyone in the facility.

The MDS nurse

In any Medicare- and/or Medicaid-certified facility, the MDS nurse is a key position. Depending on the characteristics and level of professional competence of the individual in the position and depending on the job description, this position can be a key component in attaining accuracy of MDS data and compliance with related regulations. Conversely, regardless of how good other operational systems are, if the MDS nurse does not maintain compliance with regulations, MDS data will not be accurate and the facility will be open to deficiencies related to timing, scheduling, and other compliance issues.

Job description

Job descriptions for MDS nurses are almost as varied as the nurses themselves. Sometimes the MDS nurse is responsible only for the MDS sections that are primarily nursing-related. Sometimes the job description requires the nurse to code other items as well.

RAPs usually are part of the MDS nurse's job description, but the extent of that responsibility varies. MDS nurses also generally have some responsibility at least for initial care planning, but in some facilities, this nurse completes all of the care planning.

In general, though, MDS nurse positions tend to have some job duties in common. Except in facilities where MDS completion and coordination is assigned to supervisors or nurses on the floor, MDS nurses usually are responsible for completing the portions of the MDS that focus primarily on nursing issues. Additionally, they usually complete the corresponding RAPs and resulting care plans.

Even though they may not be responsible for MDS sections assigned to other disciplines, MDS nurses typically coordinate the efforts of interdisciplinary team members, monitor the use of a common ARD for each assessment, and make sure assessments are done in a timely fashion. MDS nurses also facilitate interdisciplinary communication and help identify discrepancies in documentation and resolve such inconsistencies. Identifying the need for off-cycle assessments also usually falls into the MDS nurse's job description.

In addition, MDS nurses often have added duties that are not directly related to the MDS position. Some examples include responsibility for care plan conferences, participation in morning stand-up meetings and rehab meetings, case management of PPS and residents, case management of residents covered by health maintenance organizations, obtaining physician signatures on certification forms, infection control or staff development responsibilities, and back-up for the floor nurses.

These variations in job responsibilities and job designs are not necessarily problematic, but the MDS nurse job description should be developed with an awareness of the amount of time required to complete each task. For example, in designing these positions, the amount of time the nurse will require to complete the OBRA-mandated RAI process and PPS-required assessments often is underestimated. Therefore, although research data is not currently available, a review of several informal surveys indicates that the following represents the average time to complete the various assessments:

- **5 hours** for each comprehensive assessment, including time for data collection via interviews, record review, and direct observation, as well as RAPs and care planning for nursing-related items only
- **1.8–2 hours** for full assessment (no RAPS or care planning)
- **1 hour** for the Medicare PPS Assessment Form (MPAF)
- **1.25 hours** for each quarterly assessment (including updating the care plan)

One practical method for calculating the number of MDS nurse hours needed for a facility is to use data from the state system or reports available via the facility's MDS software to determine the number of assessments completed, by type, in the previous year. To project the hours needed for one year, adjust the historical figures for any projected changes in admission and discharge patterns and then multiply them by the amount of time needed per assessment. This number can be used to determine hours per week, per month, etc. As other tasks and meetings are added to the job description, add to the MDS hours the amount of time required for each until a grand total can be calculated.

Over the years, many providers have found that if MDS accuracy became a problem in the facility, determining whether the MDS nurse had enough time to complete the duties assigned was a good place to start looking for the problem.

Job characteristics

When the RAI process was first used circa 1990, nurses responsible for the process focused on their own responsibilities, often working almost in isolation. Since that time, with the evolution of the MDS as an instrument central to the survey process, the payment system, and quality monitoring for facilities and consumers, the MDS nurse's role has evolved as well. Today, hiring a person who has the characteristics that are important to the job is a key factor in achieving success—and in minimizing frustration for the nurse and for the interdisciplinary and administrative teams. Thus, a thorough evaluation of the job description should help to reveal the characteristics that are important to the job in the particular facility.

MDS nurses today coordinate the interdisciplinary team to ensure that the finished MDS reflects compliance with all regulations. These nurses guide negotiations about coding decisions when different disciplines see the resident differently. They also spend considerable time interacting with residents, families, and facility staff. For these reasons, their clinical capabilities, negotiating ability, and customer service skills all are as central to achieving MDS accuracy as is their technical knowledge of the instrument and related instructions.

Thus, the MDS nurse should be a self-starter with a strong clinical background, effective critical thinking skills, and at least six months of SNF experience. Other key skills include being detail-oriented but flexible enough to understand the importance of adjusting to internal facility changes as well as external changes triggered by changes in regulations.

Additionally, the MDS nurse must have an ongoing willingness and ability to learn. He or she should be a team player who can see the broader picture from the facility perspective and who can avoid territoriality when interfacing with interdisciplinary team members. Needless to say, diplomacy is a skill from which this position can significantly benefit.

Staff competence

Another key factor in the accuracy and compliance of MDS assessments is competence of each staff member with a part in the process. Competency in conducting and analyzing clinical assessments is basic to the job duties of all interdisciplinary team members, but it is critical in this context specifically because MDS assessments are based on underlying clinical assessments. This competency should already be verified through the process of reference checks on hire and through direct observation and skill evaluation during the probationary period after hire. MDS process competency evaluation should be incorporated into these pre-existing processes.

The goal is not necessarily to eliminate as a candidate-for-hire a social worker, for example, who lacks MDS competency; however, the prospective employer must understand the extent of training needed in that area at the outset of employment. Any lag time in providing such training can result in problems with accuracy of assessments transmitted to the state or submitted to the fiscal intermediary.

Interdisciplinary teams

One useful tool for assessing MDS training needs is the competency evaluation. On hire, interdisciplinary team members should be formally tested to determine how well they understand the regulations and how competent they are in filling out the form. The test could ask the new employee to collect data on a current resident and to fill out sections of the MDS related to his or her discipline. Then, a formal evaluation of the new employee's work should be undertaken by someone in the organization and designated by the administrator, who has the requisite knowledge and skill to evaluate the work. If deficiencies are identified in the coding or in related tasks, an action plan for improvement should be developed with the employee, along with a deadline for achieving competence.

In addition to assessing competency on hire, providers should conduct competency testing of all interdisciplinary team members annually. Issues selected for testing should include new or updated regulations related to the employee's job description and areas identified as high risk for errors.

MDS coordinator competency

For the MDS nurse, competency testing on hire should be more structured and formal than for other interdisciplinary team members. Figure 5.1 is an example of such a test.

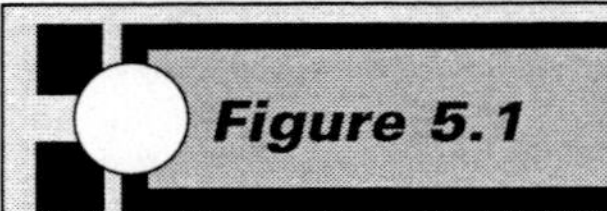

MDS competency evaluation

Name (Print) ______________________________ Date ___________

Facility ______________________________

1. The ARD for an annual assessment is 3/6/2004.
   a. The assessment must be completed at the latest 366 days from the date at section VB2 on the most recent comprehensive assessment.
   b. The first day that staff may sign off their sections as completed is 3/6/2004.
   c. The first day the RNAC may sign off the MDS as complete is the day all sections are signed off as completed.
   d. The last day the MDS may be signed off as complete is 3/20/2000 (ARD + 14 days).
   e. The last day the care plan may be signed off as complete is VB2 + 7 days.
   f. The last day for transmitting this MDS is VB4 + 31 days.
2. For a 60-day MDS
   a. The ARD must be set between day 50 and day 64.
   b. R2b must be signed by when? Within 14 days of the ARD.
   c. If the 60-day assessment also is an annual, Vb2 must be signed by when? Within 14 days of the ARD.
3. A resident is admitted 3/1/2004. The resident is discharged on 3/14/2004. What parts of the RAI process must be completed? None.
4. A resident was admitted on 3/1/2004. Her 5-day/admission assessment was completed, and she was discharged to the hospital 1 week after admission. She is expected to return in 3 weeks. She will be covered under Part A.
   a. What is the correct Discharge Tracking Form? Discharged, Return Anticipated.
   b. Is a re-entry form required when she returns? Yes.
   c. Is a significant change assessment required? Only if her status meets requirements for SCSA.

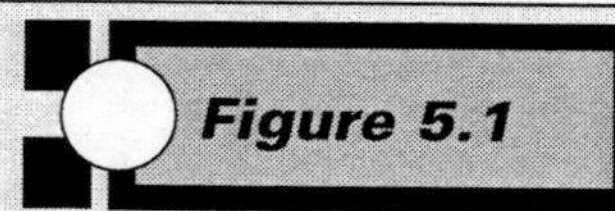

MDS competency evaluation (cont.)

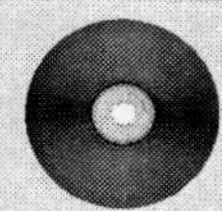

d. What will the MDS schedule be on her return? SCSA if required, Medicare Return/Readmission on admission; Quarterly at 90 days based on original admission assessment date (if SCSA not required).

5. A resident is discharged to a board and care (B&C) facility after 2 years and 1 month in the facility. Facility staff doubt he will be able to handle the lower level of care. He is readmitted after a 2-month stay in at the B&C.
   a. What is the correct discharge tracking form? Discharged Return Not Anticipated
   b. Is a re-entry form required? No.
   c. What will the MDS schedule be? Initial admission assessment.
6. For the MDS in question #1, for what time period would supporting chart documentation be required? 2/28/2001 to 3/6/2001 for the 7-day observation periods. For other observation periods, from the ARD, count backwards the number of days in the observation period.
7. What are the requirements that trigger a significant change of status assessment? Major change that is not self-limiting; impacts on more than one area of the resident's health status; requires interdisciplinary review or revision of the care plan.
8. Mrs. R. is receiving trazodone for insomnia. How is it coded in O4? Antidepressant.
9. What is the definition of fecal impaction for MDS purposes? Hard stool on rectal exam; stool seen on abdominal x-ray in sigmoid colon or higher.
10. The best person to code Section G is the Interdisciplinary Team.
11. In counting physician orders for Section P8 to justify skilled services, you would include (check all that apply):
    ___ Admission orders
    ___ Renewal orders
    _X_ New orders
    ___ Clarification orders
    ___ Sliding scale orders each time they are used
12. For a resident with a tube feeding, what supporting documentation would you expect to find in the chart? Physician orders; accurate I&O; licensed documentation of administration of tube feeding; dietary notes supporting the need for tube feeding; appropriate care plan.

MDS competency evaluation (cont.)

True/False

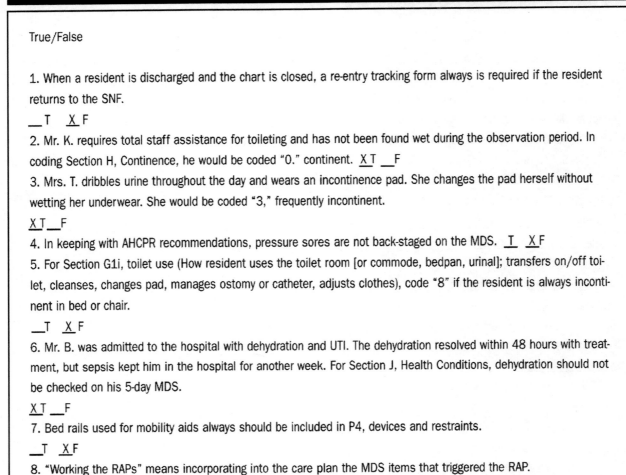

1. When a resident is discharged and the chart is closed, a re-entry tracking form always is required if the resident returns to the SNF.

__T X F

2. Mr. K. requires total staff assistance for toileting and has not been found wet during the observation period. In coding Section H, Continence, he would be coded "0." continent. X T __F

3. Mrs. T. dribbles urine throughout the day and wears an incontinence pad. She changes the pad herself without wetting her underwear. She would be coded "3," frequently incontinent.

X T __F

4. In keeping with AHCPR recommendations, pressure sores are not back-staged on the MDS. T X F

5. For Section G1i, toilet use (How resident uses the toilet room [or commode, bedpan, urinal]; transfers on/off toilet, cleanses, changes pad, manages ostomy or catheter, adjusts clothes), code "8" if the resident is always incontinent in bed or chair.

__T X F

6. Mr. B. was admitted to the hospital with dehydration and UTI. The dehydration resolved within 48 hours with treatment, but sepsis kept him in the hospital for another week. For Section J, Health Conditions, dehydration should not be checked on his 5-day MDS.

X T __F

7. Bed rails used for mobility aids always should be included in P4, devices and restraints.

__T X F

8. "Working the RAPs" means incorporating into the care plan the MDS items that triggered the RAP.

__T X F

9. When a resident falls into the Rehab High category, his therapy minutes should not exceed 325.

__T X F

10. A significant factor in RUG reimbursement is signs and symptoms of depression.

X T __F

Source: Rena R. Shephard, RRS Healthcare Consulting Services. Used with permission.

With the ever-increasing complexity of the MDS and PPS systems, it is no longer sufficient for the outgoing MDS coordinator to train the incoming nurse. In fact, this method of training can result in significant survey and reimbursement problems for the facility. Therefore, for experienced MDS coordinators who are new to the facility, providers should require not just testing but also evidence of recently received formal training in all aspects of the RAI and MDS processes. This training should have been provided by organizations or individuals with recognized expertise in this area. If the newly hired MDS nurse has not received training, provide it as soon as possible.

Once the newly hired MDS coordinator's competency has finally been established, the training must not stop there. With all of the updates and changes that occur to the MDS coding rules and related regulations, the facility must ensure that the nurse has easy access to industry sources that provide these updates. Therefore, MDS coordinators should have access to the CMS Web site for the MDS Version 2.0 at *www.cms.hhs.gov/NursingHomeQualityInits/* and to the SNF PPS Web site at *www.cms.hhs.gov/snfpps/01_overview.asp.*

The Web sites of the national healthcare associations, their state affiliates, and the American Association of Nurse Assessment Coordinators at *www.aanac.org* provide up-to-date news and information pertaining to these regulations. MDS coordinators can also look to this book's publisher, HCPro, for breaking long-term care news at *www.hcpro.com/long-term-care/.* MDS coordinators should attend annual update classes as well.

To assess the individual's level of competence in working with the MDS and PPS processes, use a formal, ongoing annual competency evaluation process. The following three documents in Figures 5.2, 5.3, and 5.4 are examples of annual evaluation tools for MDS coordinators. In addition to the material contained in these tools, MDS coordinators should be evaluated with regard to any new regulations or changes that occurred in the previous year.

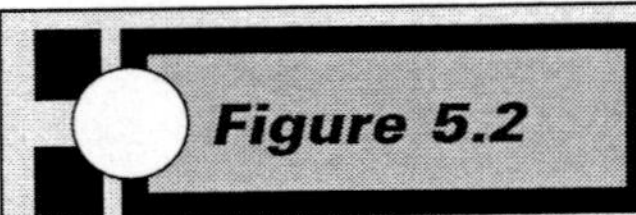

MDS coordinator competency evaluation #1

Name: ______________________ Facility: ______________________

Job category: RAI Coordinator Date: ______________________

Competency title: #1—OBRA RAI requirements

Competency statement: The RAI coordinator will demonstrate proficiency in coordinating completion of the RAI per federal regulations.

Performance criteria	Evaluation method	Not met	Met	Action plan if not met
1. Sets assessment reference date (ARD) appropriately for OBRA v. PPS requirements.	1. Supervisor review of ___ records per quarter.			
2. Completes MDSs within regulatory time frames.	2. Supervisor review of ___ records per quarter.			
3. Identifies and acts on the need for significant change MDS per regulations.	3. Verbal test Record review of two examples.			
4. Correctly utilizes discharge and reentry tracking forms.	4. Verbal test Record review of two examples.			
5. Completes a comprehensive assessment under the correct circumstances.	5. Verbal test Record review of two examples.			
6. Correctly defines ARD, completion date, care plan decision date, and transmission deadline.	6. Verbal test			
7. Demonstrates ability to correctly encode and transmit MDSs with minimal errors.	7. Supervisor review of validation reports.			
8. Demonstrates understanding of correct completion of Sections E, G, M,O, P, and T.	8. Quality review of ___ records per quarter.			
9. Completes RAP analysis utilizing critical thinking to identify causative and risk factors, complications, and need for referrals to ancillary depts.	9. Quality review of ___ records per quarter.			

All of the above performance criteria have been successfully met.

Evaluator title: ______________________ **Evaluator signature:** ______________________

Comments: ______________________ **Employee signature:** ______________________

____

____

____

____

____

Source: Rena R. Shephard, RRS Healthcare Consulting Services. Used with permission.

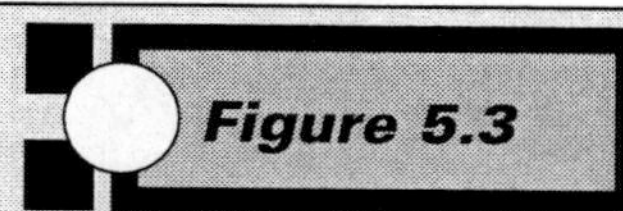

MDS coordinator competency evaluation #2

Name: ______________________ Facility: ______________ Date: __________

Job category: RAI coordinator

Competency title: # 2—PPS RAI and Medicare requirements

Competency statement: RAI Coordinator will demonstrate proficiency in the requirements of PPS with regard to MDS completion and Medicare A coverage.

Performance criteria	Evaluation method	Not met	Met	Action plan if not met
1. Correctly sets ARD to capture actual intensity of services provided.	1. Supervisor review of ___ records per quarter.			
2. Completes OMRAs per regulations.	2. Verbal test Record review of two examples			
3. Understands the correct utilization of Sections P & T.	3. Verbal test Quality review of ___ records per quarter			
4. Coordinates the completion of PPS-required MDSs per mandated schedule.	4. Verbal test Quality review of ___ records per quarter			
5. Correctly codes Section A8, Reasons for assessment.	5. Verbal test Record review of four examples			
6 Correctly codes A8 and correctly sets ARDs when the same MDS fulfills OBRA and PPS requirements.	6. Verbal test			
7. Demonstrates proficiency in MDS correction policy.	7. Verbal test			
8. Effectively communicates with billing office.	8. Supervisor review of documents			
9. Captures skilled coverage needs on MDS and ensures that supporting documentation is in chart.	9. Quality review of ___ records per quarter			
10. Ensures denial of coverage when resident no longer requires skilled coverage.	10. Verbal test with two examples			

All of the above performance criteria have been successfully met.

Evaluator title: ______________________ **Evaluator signature:** ______________________

Comments: Employee signature: ______________________

____

____

____

____

____

Source: Rena R. Shephard, RRS Healthcare Consulting Services. Used with permission.

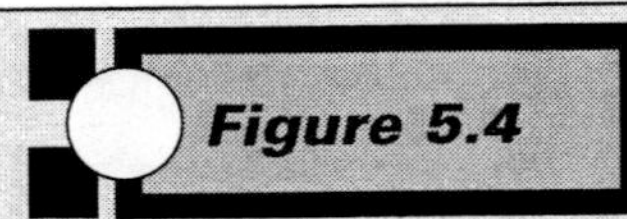

MDS coordinator competency evaluation #3

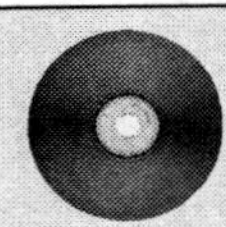

Name: ______________________ Facility: ______________________ Date:______________________

Job category: RAI coordinator

Competency title: #3—Coordination of interdisciplinary team (IDT)

Competency statement: The RAI coordinator will effectively interact with and integrate the IDT to facilitate the PPS process and quality resident care.

Performance criteria	Evaluation method	Not met	Met	Action plan if not met
1. Provides clear, convenient, accurate, timely information to IDT re: MDS schedules.	1. Supervisor observation of communication system.			
2. Promptly notifies IDT when a significant change MDS is initiated.	2. Supervisor observation of notification system.			
3. Monitors input into each MDS to ensure accuracy and consistency of responses across the interdisciplinary assessments, acting as a facilitator to help resolve disagreements.	3. Quality review of ___ records per quarter.			
4. Mentors and teaches nursing and ancillary staff to ensure that all team members are aware of and competent in their roles in the RAI and PPS processes.	4. Supervisor observation with documented examples.			
5. Coordinates and facilitates interdisciplinary resident care plan conferences per facility policy.	5. Quality review of ___ records per quarter. Supervisor observation with documented examples.			
6. Active participation in and facilitation of development of comprehensive, individualized, interdisciplinary care plan for each resident.	6. Supervisor review of __ records per quarter.			
7. Actively interacts with IDT in routine UR rounds to evaluate resident's status and needs relative to Medicare skilled needs and RUG category changes.	7. Supervisor observation with documented examples.			

All of the above performance criteria have been successfully met.

Evaluator title: ______________________ Evaluator signature: ______________________

Comments: Employee signature: ______________________

____

____

____

____

Source: Rena R. Shephard, RRS Healthcare Consulting Services. Used with permission.

Documentation systems

Accurate coding of the MDS relies upon a considerable amount of chart documentation. Regulations do not require that MDS assessment responses be duplicated elsewhere in the chart for most MDS items. However, documentation should generally be consistent with and supportive of MDS responses.

Providers continue to struggle with the question of how to ensure that needed information appears in the chart without adding unnecessary layers of time-consuming documentation. Some of the methods employed include flow sheets, check-off sheets, narrative notes, and charting by exception.

Whatever method a facility selects, the requirements for supporting documentation generally do not entail any more or less documentation than is required by the standard of practice. For example, for a resident with a pressure ulcer, the standard of practice requires that the wound be assessed periodically, care and treatment related to the ulcer be documented, and the resident's response to that care and treatment appear in the clinical record. This documentation also will support the MDS coding of the ulcer and related issues.

Another example is ADL status as represented on the MDS in Section G.1. Providers across the country have struggled to implement nursing assistant flow sheets that mimic Section G1, providing training on the coding rules to facility staff. Despite their efforts, however, many providers report that the accuracy of the ADL data is still not reaching acceptable standards.

Perhaps the most effective approach is to go back to the standard of practice requirements and rebuild the documentation system from there. For instance, as a standard of nursing practice, licensed nurses, in conjunction with rehabilitation therapists, sometimes determine the baseline ADL status of their residents. They do so to develop appropriate care plans and to supervise nursing assistants appropriately in their care of the residents.

Once the baseline is established and communicated to caregivers, documentation as specific as the Section G1 requirements is not necessary unless the resident experiences a change in ADL status. In that case, the nursing assistant who identifies the status change would be expected by the standard of practice to notify the licensed nurse in charge of the resident. That nurse, in turn, would be expected to conduct and document an assessment of the resident's status to develop interventions to help the resident attain or maintain the highest possible level of function. That documentation, including assessment findings, any physician notification, physician orders, and care plan updates, would meet the standard of practice and also would support MDS coding.

For providers who seek to reduce the time that licensed nurses must spend on documentation or who have identified a need to improve the content of the documentation, flow sheets might be helpful. Because the standard of practice requires that certain information be documented in the clinical record when, for example, an acute change of condition occurs, a flow sheet can ensure that the assessments conducted and documented by the nurses meet the standard. At the same time, the flow sheet will provide important information for coding the MDS. A sample of such a flow sheet for respiratory assessments appears in Figure 5.5.

Data collection

A facility's requirements for data collection in the process of making MDS coding decisions are key to the accuracy of the MDS data. As the *Long Term Care Facility Resident Assessment Instrument User's Manual* emphasizes, information must be collected from all available sources before coding the MDS.

For most MDS items, information must be gathered from all shifts and all disciplines for the entire observation period. In addition, all of the disciplines involved with the resident should interview the resident, family members, and others who come into contact with the resident to get their input on the issues that the various disciplines address via the MDS and RAPs. Significant errors can be identified by surveyors and fiscal intermediaries when the medical record contains information that was not used for MDS coding.

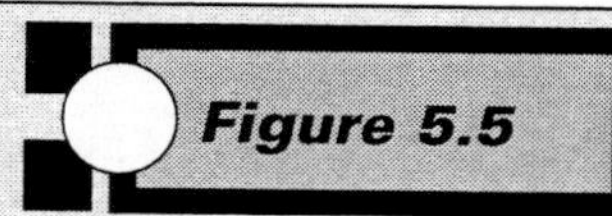

Figure 5.5 Respiratory assessment flowsheet

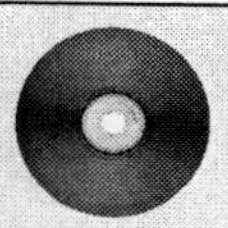

Name:______________________ Room number:______________ Medical record number:____________

Follow facility policies regarding changes of condition if any changes or abnormalities are identified

Date:													
Time:													
Oxygen saturation:													

Breath sounds: Check all that apply and document abnormalities on back

Clear													
Crackles													
Rhonchi													
Wheezes													

Secretions: Check one

Small:													
Moderate:													
Large:													
None:													
Comments:													

Mental status: Check all that apply

Awake:													
Alert:													
Responsive:													
Lethargic:													
Combative:													
Confused:													
Restless:													
Anxious:													

Breathing pattern: Check all that apply

Normal:													
Shallow:													
Labored:													
Cough:													

Skin: Check all that apply

Warm:													
Cool:													
Dry:													
Diaphoretic:													
Color WNL:													
Pale:													
Cyanotic:													

Nurse's initials													

Comment on back regarding any abnormal findings and physician notifications

Nurses' signatures: ______________________ ______________________

______________________ ______________________

Source: Rena R. Shephard, RRS Healthcare Consulting Services. Used with permission

The data collection steps outlined in the *Long Term Care Facility Resident Assessment Instrument User's Manual* include the following:

- Review the resident's record
- Communicate with and observe the resident
- Communicate with direct care staff
- Communicate with licensed professionals
- Communicate with the resident's physician
- Communicate with the resident's family

The interdisciplinary method

Another organizational process that contributes significantly to the accuracy of the MDS and compliance with related regulations is the system set up for collecting relevant data and for arriving at coding decisions. In many facilities, each discipline is assigned specific MDS sections and RAPs to complete. Figure 5.6 shows a typical breakdown of the assignments.

Figure 5.6 **The MDS by discipline**

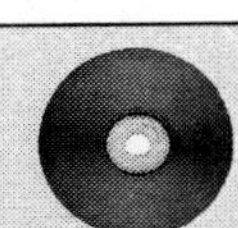

Discipline	MDS sections
Activities	N
Business office	AA, A
Dietary	K
Medical records	I
Nursing	AB, AC, D, G, H, J, L, M, O, P (except P1b), R
Social services	E, F, Q
Speech therapy	B, C (rehab residents only; otherwise, nursing)
Physical therapy/occupational therapy/speech language pathology—P1b.	T

This system can be very successful or it can be a recipe for disaster, depending on how the process is designed in the facility because the MDS and RAP processes were developed as true interdisciplinary processes, with many of the items requiring input from a broad range of individuals involved with the resident. Consequently, facility processes that foster territoriality and that compartmentalize the different MDS sections by discipline are also likely to breed inaccuracy. With such a method, each discipline conducts its clinical assessments and codes the MDS accordingly with little or no input from other disciplines or other shifts. Here are some examples of problems that result from this method:

- The social worker codes mood and behavior. The night shift reports signs and symptoms of depression, but the social worker doesn't see the report on the day shift and therefore doesn't code it on the MDS.

- The nurse coding Section G1, ADL self-performance and support provided, uses the CNA flow sheets to obtain the information for making the coding decision. The resident required more assistance with transfers and locomotion off-unit with physical therapy and occupational therapy, but because that was not reflected in the Section G1 flowsheets, the nurse did not see it and coded the resident's ADL index lower than it should have been, resulting in a lower RUG payment than the payment to which the facility was entitled.

- The fall assessment completed on admission indicated cognitive deficits, but the nurse coding the MDS did not consult the medical record in making the coding decision and therefore indicated on the MDS that the resident had none. The resident later fell because the intermittent cognitive deficits were not care planned.

On the other hand, this system can be very successful if each discipline collects information via direct observation and from all disciplines via discussion and record review. Further, the team needs to use information from the resident and family members via interview, from staff via discussion, and from the record via review before making the coding decision.

The interdisciplinary method

Another popular method for completing the MDS and RAP processes is to assign the MDS coordinator the responsibility for making all coding decisions for the MDS based on the documentation in the clinical record by all of the disciplines. Using this method, the MDS nurse conducts a thorough record review, drawing conclusions from the documentation and making the coding decisions. The problem with this method is that it bypasses important interdisciplinary discussion, analysis, and problem-solving by deferring to the nurse's perspective for all coding decisions.

The federal regulations [42 CFR 483.20(c)(1)(i)—F 278] require appropriate participation of health professionals in this process and encourage providers to include an interdisciplinary team with varied clinical backgrounds as an active part of the process. If coding inaccuracies are identified during a survey or if inappropriately analyzed RAPs failed to uncover the true nature of a resident's problems and needs with resulting harm to the resident, it might be determined that the system does not meet the regulatory requirements.

The coordination method

Processes that seem to be most effective are the ones in which the MDS coordinator truly coordinates the process. In this method, the nurse pulls together all of the information needed to make coding decisions—from record reviews, observations, and interviews—and stimulates discussion with the interdisciplinary team members regarding MDS items and other issues that need the team's input. In this way, the nurse might go into a team meeting with an idea of how an item in question should be coded, but he or she may hold a different opinion by the time the meeting ends. With this system, the MDS coordinator also would ensure that the overall medical record supports the decisions made by the team, encouraging team members to supplement their existing documentation as appropriate.

Communication

For the complex and interdisciplinary RAI, MDS, and PPS processes to be effective, collaboration and effective communication are essential. Facility processes that foster these working conditions should be developed with input from all of the stakeholders. In this way, the needs of the individual team members can be addressed, as can the needs of the team as a whole.

Some of the methods that are used for this purpose are discussed below. Some facilities use one or two of these methods; others use all of them.

Daily 'stand-up meetings'

Each morning at the start of the day, all of the interdisciplinary team members and the administrative team gather for a brief meeting. Agendas vary by facility, but these meetings all communicate important information in a concise manner to those who need it. They generally also allow for focused problem-solving of issues raised at the meeting.

The agenda generally includes a review from the previous 24 hours of admissions and discharges, falls, new weight losses, new pressure ulcers, other such incidents from the 24-hour report book at the nurses' stations, and residents with new orders for restraints. Brief updates regarding residents currently on Medicare Part A coverage are often on the agenda. These meetings also can be forums to discuss residents in the context of MDS coding decisions.

Weekly rehab meetings

These meetings, which are an industry standard, are valuable sources of information regarding the status of residents who are on Part A coverage and receiving therapy. In many facilities, HMO-covered residents are reviewed as well. Much information for the MDS and the subsequent claim form can be gleaned from these meetings.

Care plan conferences

Care plan conferences often are used to hash out MDS coding decisions for items that are not straightforward for particular residents. However, by the time of the care plan conference, the initial MDS already has been completed. Therefore, it may not be good practice to wait for the care plan conference to discuss certain issues.

Medicare case managers

For organizations that have case managers, MDS nurses generally can rely on them for up-to-date and accurate input regarding some of the MDS coding decisions. The reason is that case managers generally stay well-informed about residents' functional and medical status because of the status' relationship to skilled coverage.

Written communications among disciplines

Although face-to-face communication generally is most effective, facilities must have systems in place to facilitate written communication among disciplines. The system can be as simple as writing e-mails or placing written notes in mailboxes at the nurses' station. It is often very helpful to have an interdisciplinary communication log in a central location where team members can communicate with each other and, at the same time, maintain a record of the communications.

In conclusion

Whatever methods of communication are selected by a facility, the key is to ensure that everyone has access to the information they need to provide appropriate care and documentation. When it comes to discrepancies in clinical record documentation as they relate to MDS coding or skilled coverage, the key is to resolve disputes collaboratively—both "sides" might actually clinically be right, but the MDS coding decision must be based on the coding rules.

